Say It
With
Love

SAY IT WITH LOVE

HOWARD G. HENDRICKS
with Ted Miller

While this book is intended for the reader's personal enjoyment and profit, it is also intended for group study. A leader's guide with Reproducible Response Sheets is available from your local bookstore or from the publisher.

VICTOR BOOKS®
A DIVISION OF SCRIPTURE PRESS PUBLICATIONS INC.
USA CANADA ENGLAND

Unless otherwise indicated, Scripture quotations are from the *Authorized Version (King James)*. Other quotations are from the *New American Standard Bible* (NASB), © the Lockman Foundation 1960, 1962, 1963, 1968, 1971, 1972, 1973, 1975, 1977; *The Living Bible* (TLB) © 1971, Tyndale House Publishers, Wheaton, IL 60189; and *The Modern Language Bible: The Berkeley Version in Modern English* (MLB), © 1945, 1959, 1969 by Zondervan Publishing House. All quotations used by permission.

Twenty-second printing, 1989

Library of Congress Catalog Card Number: 72-77011
ISBN: 0-89693-676-7

Recommended Dewey Decimal Classification: 248.5
Suggested Subject Heading: WITNESS BEARING

CONTENTS

FOREWORD

Howard Hendricks is a man of God and a communicator. *Say It with Love* is primarily a book about communication—"the art and joy of telling the Good News." The author makes clear, however, that communication involves far more than mere telling or talking.

Like his speaking—and he is one of my favorite speakers—Howard Hendricks' writing is fast-paced, exciting, humorous, and packed with challenging and provocative content. I found it difficult to put down the manuscript of *Say It with Love*.

For many years, Dr. Hendricks has been one of our most popular guest speakers at Arrowhead Springs and at various other Campus Crusade for Christ sessions, including training institutes for evangelism for students, pastors, and laymen. Thousands who have heard him at these institutes—as well as multitudes of others across America—have been entertained, challenged, inspired, and motivated to action by his messages.

One of the most refreshing things about Howard Hendricks is his honesty. He dares to look at things as they are and forces us to confront reality with him. The results are sometimes discomfiting, but the discomfiture is of the variety that gets us moving off dead center.

In *Say It with Love,* Dr. Hendricks reveals what communication with others is all about. The message we have to communicate is all-important, and nobody knows that better than this Dallas Seminary professor of Christian Education. But knowing the message is only the beginning. The author impresses us with the absolute necessity of *caring* about the Lord and His message and of *living* the message.

There are many obstacles to effective communication, and these are exposed and dealt with, always in a colorful and effective manner. The chapter "Training Communicators" is so full of solid, sensible, straight-from-the-Bible principles, that it alone could radically alter the reader's concepts forever.

Because no principles are any better than the people who try to implement them, *Say It with Love* has a major section on "Living the Message." Beginning with the individual's personal life with God, this section gets down to earth about relationships: with our mates, our children, and others, including people in our churches, neighborhoods, and the marketplace.

Of the many elements necessary for good communication, none is more important than love. "If I speak with the tongues of men and of angels, but do not have love, I have become a noisy gong or a clanging cymbal" (1 Cor. 13:1, NASB). In emphasizing the need to speak with love, Dr. Hendricks stresses the importance of "loving in deed"—of showing those whom we would help by our *deeds* that we truly love them. Such love can be better communicated by deeds than by mere words.

This book is a happy example of what it purports to teach. It is written with obvious joy and will be read with joy; its artistry will be worked out in many lives for years to come. I commend *Say It with Love* with the prayer that, as a result of reading it, the reader will be better able to experience and share the abundant life of our living Lord.

BILL BRIGHT
President
Campus Crusade for Christ International

San Bernardino, California
May 1, 1972

8

DON'T FAKE IT
AUTHOR'S PREFACE

One thing we do not need today is another voice giving directions. Man in the late twentieth century is confused in the traffic of life. He is like the young country boy downtown in the big city for the first time. He is bewildered by the changing lights and the commanding arrows. He is terrified by the frantic streets, and in the midst of the confusion he is lonely. More than anything else he wants to be loved.

Do you remember the fairy tale of the ugly toad who was really a handsome prince? All he needed to break the spell of the wicked witch was a kiss from a beautiful maiden. But what beautiful maiden would stop to kiss an ugly toad? Obviously, only one who stopped first to talk to him and get to know him.

We who wear the beauty of Jesus Christ through His grace pass by many frightened, lost, ugly souls. A hurried, superficial touch of courtesy cannot convey a message of love. It can only begin. Love moves into the realm of need, flows into a life to share remedies.

Four starving lepers crouched in the shadows of an ancient Israelite town beseiged by the marauding Syrians. Since they were dying anyway, they decided to go into the Syrian camp and beg for food. Perhaps someone would show mercy. When they arrived, they saw an incredible sight. The camp was deserted, hastily abandoned when God sent a sound like that of an approaching army. All the food and supplies were intact. The beggars began to eat and hoard the riches with no thought of their starving people.

"We are not doing right," said one of them. "This is a day of good news, but we are keeping silent" (2 Kings 7:9, NASB).

Could these words be said of Christians today? In a spirit of love and concern we must tell the good news that Christ died

9

for sinners, and that He arose again to live for them. This is our day of opportunity, and the world today is more ready to listen and to respond to this message than many Christians are to share it. We invalidate the message of God's love for men when we do not love men for God.

Mr. Ted Miller of Wheaton, Illinois has applied the pencil and scissors and paste of his editing skills to the chapters of this volume, an effort for which I am deeply grateful.

It is for you, my readers, to place these concepts into the sandals of your own private march for Jesus Christ. As you go for God, be sure you *Say It with Love.*

HOWARD G. HENDRICKS
Dallas Theological Seminary
Dallas, Texas

OUR MESSAGE

Part 1

GOD SAID IT WITH LOVE

Chapter One

Memories of my childhood haunt me. My Roman Catholic mother and my agnostic father were separated before I was born, and most of my childhood was spent with my paternal grandmother. If I look back into the dim recesses of my memory, I can see a boy going from tavern to tavern in Philadelphia, picking up pretzels to eat along the way, looking for an alcoholic grandfather to see if he could slip the pay envelope out of the old man's back pocket before he shot the whole wad in the tavern.

The fact that an unhappy boy with a miserable beginning like that not only has something going for his own life today but also has something worth sharing with students and others across the country is testimony to the fact of God's love for the unlovely. Man, with the environment I grew up in, I was a little brat! But God changed it all!

The Living Bible says it so well: "When we were utterly helpless with no way of escape, Christ came at just the right time and died for us sinners who had no use for Him" (Rom. 5:6). The entire chapter spells out that love. "Even if we were good, we really wouldn't expect anyone to die for us, though, of course, that might be barely possible. But God showed His great love for us by sending Christ to die for us while we were still sinners" (Rom. 5:7-8).

That's the wonder of the Gospel—that God, in love, broke into human history and made a way where there was no way. The Gospel, as expressed in 1 Corinthians 15:3-4, is the news that "Christ died for our sins according to the Scriptures, and that He was buried, and that He rose again the third day according to the Scriptures." What astounding news! Christ, the God-Man, acted to rescue a race of creatures that had turned against their Creator!

But it isn't enough that God has provided such a wonderful salvation. Man is still lost until he accepts the gift of eternal life. And in his lost condition, he is running from God so hard that God can scarcely get close enough to tell him the Good News. Man knows down deep that all he deserves from a righteous and holy God is judgment, and he just cannot believe that God is seeking him out of love.

One of the first things Adam and Eve did after they ate the forbidden fruit was to run and hide from God among the trees of the garden. That is a picture of guilt. And man has been hiding from God ever since.

Some time back, newspapers carried the story of a young fellow named William, who was a fugitive from the police. The teenager had run away with his girlfriend because the parents had been trying to break them up. What William didn't know was that an ailment he had been seeing the doctor about was diagnosed, just after his disappearance, as cancer.

Now, here was William, doing his best to elude the police, lest he lose his love, while they were doing their best to find him, lest he lose his life. He thought they were after him to punish him; they were really after him to save him. William is representative of every man, whose guilt tells him God is after him to straightjacket him in this life and torture him forever.

Jesus went out of His way to correct that impression. After

giving the world the great, immortal words of John 3:16, "God so *loved* the world that He gave His only begotten Son," Jesus went on to declare, "God did not send His Son into the world to condemn it, but to save it" (v. 17, TLB).

The entire New Testament is a record of the continuing entreaty of the Lord toward a world He had already died to redeem. God didn't just *say,* "Be saved"; He said it with the highest degree of love.

I know a young preacher who reacted, as many have, to the lengthy altar calls sometimes given in churches. To him, such altar calls demeaned the Gospel. "Why should we plead and coax and beg people to get saved," he said. "When I present the Gospel, I am doing people a favor. I am giving them the most wonderful opportunity in the world. I'll preach the message and give the opportunity. Then, if they want to come, let them come; I'm certainly not going to beg them."

Then one day God slapped him right across the face with a passage in 2 Corinthians 5. ("Thanks, Lord, I *needed* that!" he said.) The verse read, "Now then we are ambassadors for Christ, *as though God did beseech you* by us: we pray you in Christ's stead, be ye reconciled to God" (v. 20).

He saw that here the great, almighty, and transcendent God was pictured as beseeching, pleading with, begging sinners to be reconciled to Him. After God provided the way of salvation, He had not told sinners, in effect, "There it is; take it or leave it." He had not simply "said it," but He had said it—was still saying it—with love.

I don't know what he did about the altar call problem, but he certainly had a new attitude! He had caught a glimpse of God's matchless love.

LOVE—THE GREATEST FORCE

Has it ever occurred to you that love is the greatest positive force in existence? People respond to love. Jesus said, "And I, if I be lifted up from the earth, will draw all men unto Me" (John 12:32).

He was referring to the drawing power of the Cross—the drawing power of the love that made Him die "for us sinners who had no use for Him."

The Cross contradicts our sense of worthlessness and gives us hope that we can adequately respond to His love. My own public school experience illustrates that principle.

I can remember only two public schoolteachers I ever had: my fifth-grade teacher and my sixth-grade teacher. It kind of amuses me that I should be teaching, because school was just a bad-news item all the way for me. I could never get together with my schoolteachers on the basic objective of the thing. The moment they would go out of the room, I would go into action.

Finally my fifth-grade teacher, Miss Simon, tied me to my seat, my hands behind my back, with a great big rope. Then she took mucilage paper and started over my mouth and went clear around my neck. "Now, Howard," she said, "you will sit still and keep quiet." So what else could I do?

Finally I was graduated from her class, for obvious reasons, and I went on to my sixth-grade teacher. I'll never forget her: Miss Noe, 6'4" tall—sort of a feminine version of Sherlock Holmes! I used to think that if that dear woman had done nothing but just stand erect, she would have done something for me.

I walked into her class, and the first thing she said was, "Oh, you're Howard Hendricks. I've heard a lot about you." Then she jarred me by adding, "But I don't believe a word of it!"

That year I found the first teacher who ever convinced me that she believed in me. And you know, I never let that woman down. I would knock myself out for her. I'd work and do all kinds of extra projects. My most vivid memories of that class are of occasionally looking over at the door with the little windowpane in it and seeing Miss Simon, my fifth-grade teacher, peeking in to see this thing which was come to pass. Here I was, sitting, clothed, and in my right mind—and working.

The transforming power of God's love has been proved over and over. The grossest sinners have become godly saints. Self-centered wretches have been so completely captivated by His love that they have willingly laid down their lives for Jesus Christ.

My home knew little of God's love, and I can still remember coming out of it. Entering into my own marriage, I prayed, "O God, I don't know what my kids will ever remember me for. I don't really care if they ever remember me as a well-known preacher or professor or writer. All I cry to You for, Lord, is that You will help them to remember me as a father who loved them."

Humanly speaking, I might never have been saved if someone hadn't "said it with love" to me. I was nine years old, a little terror. I was out playing marbles one day when a man named Walt came along and invited me to Sunday School. There was nothing appealing to me about anything with "school" in it, so he made me another proposition—one I liked a lot better. "Wanna play a game of marbles with me?" he asked.

After he'd wiped me out in a couple games of marbles, he inquired, "Wanna learn how to play this game better?"

By the time he'd taught me how to play marbles over the next few days, he'd built such a relationship with me that I'd have gone *anywhere* he suggested. You know what that meant? I ended up in his Sunday School class with a dozen other boys, most of whom he'd magnetized in very much the same way. Of the thirteen boys in that class, nine were from broken homes, and five were Roman Catholics. Eleven of those boys ended up in vocational Christian work.

Thank God for a man like Walt, who "said it with love."

PEDRO, THE CREEP

But showing such love is not always easy. Some people are awfully unlovable. Like "Pedro." He was a creep. There was no other word for it. The missionary who tells the story—Dale Bishop, of Colombia—confesses he would duck into a store and go out the back whenever he saw Pedro coming down the street.

Pedro was one of those slick sort of characters, always after a fast buck. After several contacts with him, Bishop began to despise him.

"Lord, Pedro is a hopeless, despicable man. Take him. Send him away. I simply can't stand him." At least Bishop was honest with God.

Wrestling with the problem over a period of weeks, the missionary began to see that *he* himself must change. He had to at least love Pedro "in the Lord," he recognized.

One day he greeted Pedro on the street. They talked and Pedro invited the missionary to have a Coke with him. They talked further, and Bishop began to see Pedro as a fellow human being, a man with feelings, a man for whom Christ had died.

One morning the missionary awoke and found that God had changed him. He actually *loved* Pedro—more than simply "in the Lord." While he acknowledges that they probably will never be best friends, he had *willed* to love Pedro and the love had come.

That is what we must do—*will* to love even the unlovely for Christ's sake. And that may involve a high price tag!

Sometimes our love is ambivalent. We talk love and act indifference. We are like the fourth-grade class that sent a card to their teacher who was at home recovering from surgery. The card read, "Your fourth-grade class wishes you a speedy recovery—by a vote of 15 to 14."

God is different.

God wishes us a speedy recovery from the penalty and power of sin, and He is not divided or halfhearted about it. He says to our generation, as He did to Israel of old, "As I live saith the Lord God, I have no pleasure in the death of the wicked; but that the wicked turn from his way and live. Turn ye, turn ye from your evil ways, for why will ye die, O house of Israel?" (Ezek. 33:11)

Why will ye die? That is the central question of the Gospel. That goes to the heart of our message. Because Jesus Christ died in our place on the cross, we don't have to die. This suffering world needs the Good News: "Christ also suffered. He died once for the sins of all us guilty sinners . . . that He might bring us safely home to God" (1 Peter 3:18, TLB). "He is not willing that any should perish, and He is giving more time for sinners to repent" (2 Peter 3:9, TLB).

That is our message. Really, it is *His* message.

And He said it with love.

So must we.

SHARING THE MESSAGE

Part 2

KNOWING FEELING ACTING

Chapter Two

Novelist Ayn Rand had mesmerized a student audience at Yale University with her prickly ideas. Afterward a reporter from *Time* magazine asked her, "Miss Rand, what's wrong with the modern world?"

Without hesitation she replied, "Never before has the world been so desperately asking for answers to crucial questions, and never before has the world been so frantically committed to the idea that no answers are possible.

"To paraphrase the Bible," she continued, "the modern attitude is, 'Father, forgive us, for we know not what we are doing—and *please don't tell us!*' "

It is to such a generation that God has called today's Christians to minister—in an age which sees everything that was nailed down coming loose, a time when things happen which people once thought could never happen. And God has chosen you and me to be His personal representatives to this generation. I'm sure He could have selected far more efficient means, but I hope you never recover from the fact that He has handpicked you for this mission if you are a Christian.

Perhaps you find yourself talking more these days and enjoying it less. If so, you may be on the verge of the greatest breakthrough in your Christian life and ministry. Nothing is as easy as talking; nothing is as difficult as communicating. Those to whom you and I effectively communicate are changed; they are never quite the same again. I believe communication is one of the most delicate and critical tasks ever to confront the human mind—especially communicating in the spiritual realm. Here the results affect not only time but eternity.

Our communication problem is focused clearly in 1 Corinthians 14:8-12 (TLB). "And if the army bugler doesn't play the right notes, how will the soldiers know that they are being called to battle? In the same way, if you talk to a person in some language he doesn't understand, how will he know what you mean? You might as well be talking to an empty room. I suppose that there are hundreds of different languages in the world, and all are excellent for those who understand them, but to me they mean nothing. A person talking to me in one of these languages will be a stranger to me and I will be a stranger to him. Since you are so anxious to have special gifts from the Holy Spirit, ask Him for the very best, for those that will be of real help to the whole church."

Did you ever pray for the gift of speech? There is a greater gift, and that is the gift of communication. This is what Paul longed for. The climactic thought of this paragraph is in verse 19: "Yet in the church I had rather speak five words with my understanding, that by my voice I might teach others also, than 10,000 words in an unknown tongue."

Note what he says: five words that can be understood and communicated to others—rather than 10,000 words of uncommunicative speech.

Another passage freighted with communicational significance is 2 Timothy 2:2. Here Paul says: "And the things that thou hast heard of me among many witnesses, the same commit thou to faithful men, who shall be able to teach others also." Communication is a transmission of specific meaning. Paul declared that God had revealed life-giving truths to him, and he in turn was communicating the revelation to others. Now he charges Timothy to make a deposit of those convictions in the lives of "faithful men" in such a way that they will be equipped to convey these same truths to others. It is a ministry of multiplication. Every time you communicate in the spiritual realm, you launch a process which, ideally, will never end.

Let's examine the potential of effective communication. Suppose you did nothing for the next six months but disciple a person you had led to Christ so that at the end of the training period he was equipped to teach others. In the next six months you trained another disciple, and the first one trained another convert. At the end of a year, you and three other Christians would be ready to disciple four more. At this rate of evangelism and training, the whole world would be won to Christ in eighteen years! Obviously there has been a breakdown in the Christian communication process. The failure is devastating. We must share the message of God's life to others in such a way that they can communicate it to others.

The process of communication is a highly technical matter if you take the academic approach. Most of the books on the subject are a guaranteed cure for insomnia; two pages of some books will put me into the second or third stage of anesthesia. I have tried to boil down this body of literature to a functional procedure for communicating the Gospel and commission of Christ.

The first step is what I call concept/feeling/action: these are three essential components in beginning the communication process.

MASTER THE MESSAGE
The first is a mental or intellectual component: *you must know*

something before you can communicate it, and the better you know it, the better you are able to communicate it. The *concept,* or message, is eminently important. What you believe always determines how you behave. We must master Christ's message to the world and let it master us. Chapter 1 sets forth this message—the compelling story of Good News. But we must never stop the message, for effective communication results only from the overflow of a full life. The man or woman who stops learning today stops communicating tomorrow.

Unfortunately, our greatest asset, the Christian message, sometimes becomes a great liability. In some churches, the Christian message is little more than intellectual. The correct information is thought to automatically make genuine Christians, but Jesus warned against that. He said, "Not every one that saith unto Me, Lord, Lord, shall enter into the kingdom of heaven. . . . And then will I profess unto them, I never knew you; depart from Me" (Matt. 7:21-23).

Another distortion of the message is its enshrinement in a church building. Many churches across the country are repositories of the truth, and it's as if they had a sign in front which says, "HERE WE ARE, YOU LUCKY SINNERS! WELCOME." The assumption is: "How fortunate that you can come to our church; we keep truth in a flask here, and we'll pour out a little if you'll come here every Lord's Day." I can't find a verse of Scripture that commands a lost person to go to church; I know a lot of Scripture that commands believers to go into a lost world.

Dr. James Stewart, professor of New Testament at the University of Edinburgh, described what he thought is the greatest threat to the church. He said it is not Communism, atheism, materialism, nor Catholicism; the greatest threat is Christians trying to sneak into heaven incognito without ever sharing their faith. Tragically, these people have the truth but not enough to keep them from forgetting that evangelism is the process of one beggar telling another beggar where to find bread.

FEELINGS ARE IMPORTANT

A strong grasp of the message is important, but it is not enough. Your *feeling* about the message has a lot to do with its communication.

Years ago someone asked Charles Haddon Spurgeon, "How can I communicate like you do?"

"It's very simple," he answered. "Pour some kerosene over you, light a match, and people will come to watch you burn."

That should do it! Is the Gospel message exciting to you? Does it move you the way you want it to move the listeners who have never really heard it?

You've heard of a talented rabble-rouser—some sensationalist who doesn't know what he believes—getting on his soapbox and yelling his head off. He's so committed to his thing that 150 people take off and follow him. He has captured their feelings as well as their bodies for his undefined cause.

There's another emotion that really communicates to people: it's love. Of course, love is more than a feeling, but it certainly involves our feelings. I find that the more love I show a person, the greater the impact I have on his life.

Recently our seminary had a student with some severe physical problems, and his wife became quite ill. I got involved with this student and found out where he was hurting. I said to him, "Friend, I'm going to give you some money. Don't tell anybody about this. I just want you to know that I love you, and there are no strings attached."

The student said, "Prof, you can't afford to do that."

I told him, "I feel this is what God wants me to do, so don't rob me of the privilege of giving." We became close friends as I moved from the role of professor into the role of *friend,* a Christian brother in more than name.

Another of our students put love in shoe leather after he heard a fellow student say he was going to have to drop out of school for lack of funds. They weren't especially good friends, but the first student took almost $2,000 worth of audiovisual equipment, sold it, and gave the money to the needy student. Can you imagine what that did for their friendship and for their love of God?

I think you cannot communicate in depth to a person until you love him. And the more you love him, the more you will communicate. I've wondered why people followed Jesus Christ when He was on earth, and I'm sure I don't know the full answer. But I believe more and more that a big reason was that Jesus overtly loved them. He communicated His love by the amount of time He spent with them and the concern He frequently expressed for them. Even His rebukes were offered in love. A lover is a leader, and a worthy leader is a lover.

LIVING OUT THE MESSAGE
The third component in the communication process is *action*, or behavior. We speak with our actions as well as with our words. Sometimes our actions nullify our words. When you think you have the right set of words and you feel deeply about the message, your own actions may give the lie to your words.

You know what bugs me about my children? They remind me so much of myself! My problem is not that I don't know enough—I know ten times as much as I need to know. My problem is that what I do is not always consistent with what I know, and that's why others do not read me.

Perhaps my actions are inconsistent with my words because I haven't sufficiently learned the message by practicing it.

Southern Methodist University had a professor in its School of Law whose teaching I admire greatly. In fact, I used to send my students over to watch this man in action. He would set up a courtroom scene in class with one student as the judge, a group as the jury, a prosecutor, and the defense attorney. He sat in the back, his eyes closed, and you would be convinced he was out for lunch. But he was hearing everything.

I can see him now, storming down the aisle after it's over and yelling, "Good night! You don't mean to tell me you're going to try a case like that, do you? You know what I would do with that prosecution if I were the defense? This is what I'd do. . . ." And when he gets through, there isn't anything left.

The defense is listening to all this, smiling. Then he whips around and says, "You know what I would do with the defense that you presented? This is what I'd do. . . ." And the defense crumbles. Then he winks, and he says, "Hey, men, you want to know how to win that case? Follow me." And like a Pied Piper he takes off across the campus to Lawyer's Inn where they all sit down around some Cokes and talk "trials."

This man has trained winners. Why? Because he gets beyond the realm of concepts into action. Those students of his have to live out what they've learned—live it out in situations that are as close to reality as that knowledgeable professor can make them.

One day I asked him, "What is your educational philosophy?"

"Educational philosophy?" he replied. "I don't know what you're talking about. I have only one principle of teaching, and that is I would rather have my students lose in here and win out there than win here but lose out there."

I think we Christians have too many winners in the church building while we're losing like crazy "out there." We don't need less message, but we need to put our message in action on Main Street. A lot of people out there haven't yet learned there *is* an Answer to this generation's desperate questions.

BREAKING THE SOUND BARRIERS

Chapter Three

Americans and Britishers speak the same language—or do they? When I was in England I had considerable difficulty with their curious expressions. At the airport I asked a simple enough question of the chap who was taking me to the hotel: "Should we put these bags in the trunk?"

"I beg your pardon?" he chirped.

"Shall we put these in the *trunk?*"

"Trunk? Oh, yes, I've got it. You mean the boot."

The boot? Even a Texan couldn't get them in his boot! But my education was launched. I gathered four pages of new terms in my visit to the "mother country." Somehow I mastered the terms for food and other essentials, and survived to thrive again in good old Texas.

Words are the best clothes we have for communicating, but sometimes we could wish for something better. These building blocks of language can rise into grotesque or beautiful forms. The big question is: Do they communicate the message of the speaker? This is critically important to the communicator who seeks to share the Gospel of Jesus Christ.

I spoke at a youth conference where a number of the seminary students got into a rap-session with the faculty, and we were scraping the Milky Way on a theological space trip. A teenage fellow, listening, suddenly interrupted with: "What in the world are you guys talking about?" It stopped us dead. This kid was a merit scholarship winner, and he couldn't follow us through the verbal smog.

The English language is a living thing. Like everything alive, it is constantly changing. It isn't nearly as inflexible as some people think. If a fellow insists on talking the way people talked years ago, he can soon lose touch with the current generation, for the secret of communication is to talk in the language of the people who are listening.

After one of my characteristically brilliant lectures at the seminary, a student came up and said, "Prof, that was superb, outstanding; you are certainly the most brilliant professor I've ever had. In fact, I really think you are more brilliant than Einstein."

I thought he was sort of getting carried away, but it's nice to have one fan. And then I said, "How's that?" And in so saying, I fell directly into the trap.

"Well, Prof," he said, "they say that only ten men in the world could understand Einstein. I don't think there is anyone who can understand you."

We evangelicals have a special talent for a high fog index in our speech. (I've tried to improve since the encounter with the student who floored me with his flattering remarks.) We can partly blame King James' antiquated English for the high fog index, but much of the fault is twentieth-century Christian. We haven't made the effort to translate spiritual language into everyday situations, and our Sunday jargon is forced to take a rest the other six days of the week. We need a graphic, simple language that will get a hearing in the marketplace.

Some of our words are simply too big. We're like the doctor who smiles and says, "Brace yourself. You have gastroenteritis."

"Right, Doc," we moan. "What do I really have?"

"A stomachache."

That I can understand. And spiritually sick people can understand us better if we use simple words. Certain words are vital, but they are clear only if they are explained. Such terms as *saved, redemption, propitiation, the deeper life, total depravity,* and many others belong to a specialized vocabulary which must be defined for our friends outside of Christ.

TOUCHING THE NEED

A Christian woman read in the newspaper about a car crashing into a house and killing a baby inside. She grieved over the loss to the mother and then wondered about the welfare of the errant driver, a woman. After resisting the impulse for several days, she wrote a sympathetic letter to the guilty driver and told her that God cared about her need. She included her phone number and waited.

The desolate woman called back, and after a long conversation the two strangers agreed to meet. Because of that visit and the Christian's witness to God's love, the sorrowing woman trusted Christ as her Saviour. She came to a Bible study group and to church, and the love she encountered helped bring her family members to Christ also. She had to go to jail for her involuntary crime, but her faith kept her strong and made an impact on other prisoners. The chain of blessing went on adding links because a Christian woman spoke simply and acted lovingly toward a needy individual.

To be an effective communicator we must touch the nerve of need. Scratch people where they itch.

I work often with people teaching in Sunday Schools, and it is startling to encounter teachers who know little about the needs of their children, young people, and adults.

A woman came to me at the conclusion of a convention and said, "Professor Hendricks, I teach in the Junior Department, and I'm so concerned about the socialization problem."

I said, "Yes, what is the problem?"

"Well," she said, "in the Junior Department the girls hate the boys and the boys hate the girls."

"And what's the problem?" I repeated.

"Well, I don't think they should do that," she lamented.

"Look lady, in a few years God will change that," I assured her. "When He does, you'll wish He hadn't."

Junior girls will keep junior boys away from a party, but junior-high girls are indispensable for drawing junior-high boys to a party. And the battle to get Johnny to wash behind his ears is won by a little blond at school!

A teacher of high school girls at my church came to me after I visited her class several times and asked for my evaluation. I said, "Anne, how straight do you want it? You want me to tell it like it is?"

"I really do," she replied.

"OK. Here it is. You're talking about parties and they're talking about the pill. You're talking about holding hands and they're talking about going to bed. Your task, Anne, is to get on *their* wavelength and to talk about *their* needs."

We used to read about the generation gap, but the chasms between people are actually a blur in communication. I don't think there is any more of a generation gap than there has ever been. But there is a communication gap—and that gap is widening.

MAKE THEM LISTEN

Communication, however, is always a two-way street: not only what you're doing as a speaker but what they are doing as listeners is critical. I hate to say it, but I believe most people are conditioned *not* to listen. That is, they engage in selective hearing. The whole matter is complicated, of course, by the fact that a person can listen three to ten times "as fast" as you can speak—that gives him a lot of time on his hands.

Some people only listen to things that will support their prejudices. A lot of what you say may disturb them, and so they bail out rather than think about it. Thinking can be painful—it just might change one's whole lifestyle. This bias is an almost impossible barrier, but an encouraging factor is that you usually don't have to wait long before discovering the problem. Sometimes a verbal shock treatment offers as much hope for getting through as anything for this kind of disease. But be ready for emergency resuscitation if the confrontation produces a communicative coronary.

Arthur Miller, the great playwright and critic, was asked, "How can you tell a good play?"

He replied, "When in the midst of the play I am wont to shout, 'My God, that's me!' then I know it's a gasser."

We too must sharpen the focus of our message. When I was a kid, I had a magnifying glass. A number of girls in my neighborhood used to sunbathe, and one of my impious pastimes was to maneuver that magnifying glass so it concentrated the rays of the sun directly on target. That's communication!

Listeners identify themselves in a good drama or a good message; it gets personal, and they can't help listening.

Outside circumstances always affect listeners, and you can't usually control these. But by recognizing there is always some static on the communication line, you can try to offset it.

Imagine yourself in an auditorium, perhaps a church, and a man comes in the door, walks down the aisle all the way to the platform, walks across the platform, hands a piece of paper to a man sitting there who reads it. There is a little conversation. Then he goes back across the platform and back up the aisle. Guess where the people are.

The next time this happens to me you know what I'm going to do? I'm going to say, "There is a man coming down the aisle. There he is. He's now up on the platform. He is now giving a note to Mr. Blank. Mr. Blank is reading it. He is communicating back to Schmotgot. And there he goes, back and down." Because it's a total wipeout anyway.

But there is something even more important to communication

than coping with distraction.

After class one day I stopped a student and said, "Something's bugging you, isn't it?"

"Yeah, Prof. I'm kinda shook up."

"Come over to my office," I invited.

He came over and unloaded the whole thing. We got down on our knees together and prayed about it. The next time he came back to my class the possibilities of his hearing what I had to say were increased immeasurably. He thinks of me as a person interested in him as an individual—not someone cramming an assignment down his throat.

This points up the role of timing in the process of communication. Some are not ready to hear you now, but tomorrow or two weeks from now they may be hurting so badly they are going to be searching for answers.

MORE THAN WORDS

There's another barrier—a practically invisible one—to effective communication. It's a surface, superficial response. You've probably seen it.

I had a boy in a church where I served who memorized 800 verses of Scripture. He could give them word-perfect; I could call on him for any one of the 800, and he would give it back instantly, with chapter and verse. But they were only skull-deep.

In the Junior High Department we were regularly losing some of the offerings. The record would say $1.97 given, and 95¢ would arrive. I was appointed a committee of one to look into the situation and, would you believe, the pilferer was the champion memorizer. I took him out for a Coke and hit him with a verse of Scripture about thievery—whereupon he promptly corrected my misquotation. Then I asked if he saw any connection between that Scripture and his taking the money.

He said, "No, I don't."

It is altogether possible to program words into a person's mind without affecting that person's value structure. To me as a teacher, nothing is more paralyzing. Right words must be translated into action to have value with God.

As we can have words without communication, we can also have communication without words, of course. When my children were small, they sometimes read a message from me across a room by meeting my glance. *Looks* can communicate. They called it "Dad's eagle eye."

My father was a man who said very little—I think I remember almost everything he said. (He was an Air Force colonel and very patriotic—he'd lay down stripes and I saw stars!) He communicated many things to me, including the fact that he loved me, but it was more by what he did and what he stood for than by what he said.

I can still remember, however, one basic rule he taught me verbally. Once he said, "Son, if you're late for anything, I'll send flowers for your funeral." That's the only time I ever heard him say that, but it made an impression. I knew that he was always on time, and now I don't know how to be late. Example was a very effective means of communication that made his words powerful.

But sometimes our nonverbal communication emasculates our verbal communication instead of supporting it. Perhaps you tell a new convert, "I want you to know that I love you." Maybe he thinks, *I don't believe it,* but he wouldn't say it. However, if you have spent time with this person and pulled him out of a dilemma before he broke right through the bottom, this communicates so much more than your words do.

Actions communicate.

Attitude is also very important because it tends to be infectious. A veil of superiority or negativism is quickly communicated. A student came up to me after class one day and said, "Prof, are you mad about something?"

"Oh, no, I'm really not."

"It sure comes through that way."

I started thinking, and I said, "Yeah, I really am; I'm sorry."

I hadn't realized this anger was still with me. I had to get alone with the Lord and have this thing cleared up so it didn't betray my message and my Lord.

Attitudes communicate.

The idea of employing words to transmit our thoughts seem elementary, like taking an automobile trip. We've done it often; it's become a familiar habit. But certain prerequisites must be met. We take for granted that, in order to drive from here to there, we— first of all—need a worthy car in good repair. There must be an adequate road. We must allow sufficient time. The weather must be cooperative. There must be sufficient fuel available.

Having met all these requirements, the trip is a simple matter. Similarly, communication is facilitated with the right words aimed in the right direction and supported with the understanding that guides the words aright. The language of God's Good News must travel a straight course if spiritually dead lives are to be made alive in Christ.

IMPROVING COMMUNICATIONS

Chapter Four

There are at least two ways of serving a meal. I could come to a table that is beautifully spread with T-bone steaks, mashed potatoes, parsley peas, iced tea with a slice of lemon, molded salad garnished with cheddar cheese, and cherry pie piled high with whipped cream. That is, I could if I were not dieting.

A second kind of meal can consist of one huge bowl of food served on a bare table. Suppose I ask my wife, "What is this?"

"I'm sorry, Honey," she says. "I just didn't have time to prepare the meal in the usual way, so I took the steak, the peas, the mashed potatoes, the salad, and the cherry pie, and I put them all together with the iced tea. It's the best I could do."

The meals are equally nourishing, but not equally appetizing. Our witnessing is like those two meals in some ways.

You may not be serving up verbal hash in your witnessing, but on the other hand you may not be offering a delectable spread, either. How can you improve the communication of your message? How can you add appeal as well as nourishment? One thing that will help is to identify your problems in communication. Many people fail to make progress because they are perpetuating their past failures.

ENCOURAGE QUESTIONS

What kind of questions do you get in response to your teaching or witnessing? If different people tend to ask you the same questions, you may not be getting through very well in that area. Your approach—and maybe your message—needs something different.

Or do you get questions?

If they don't ask questions, it could mean they're not interested, or perhaps your style has quashed their response before it got out.

I taught a class at school one year in which the men wouldn't get involved. I'd try to get things going—and got nothing. Finally in the middle of it I said, "Gentlemen, I want to level with you. What is the problem? I ask for questions for discussion and you won't peep."

Deathly silence. Then one student said, "You really want to know, Prof?"

"I really want to know."

He said, "We got burned in another class when a student asked a question, and the professor spun around and fried the kid in his chair. We're dumb, Prof, but we aren't stupid. We just stopped talking."

I said, "Men, I want you to know that you will never be laughed at for any question, and if I don't have the answer I'll tell you, but I want you to ask it." The whole dynamics of the class changed; I could hardly end some of our sessions.

Questions are important. Sometimes I think the only foolish questions are the unasked ones. I remember studying the Gospel of Mark in a group and a businessman said, "Hold it. Got a question for you. You don't mean to tell me that Jesus Christ is God, do you?" In the average group, a question like that would shake the church pillars—maybe even the foundations! "Good night! Who in the world is that? Who's the heretic?" they'd wonder.

In our group we made a hero out of him. "That's tremendous, Jim," I said. Here was a man who was coming to grips with the real issues. He was beginning to discover the truths that could change his life. So we encouraged him along; we didn't expect him to digest spiritual steak before he had teeth.

One of the best professors I ever had spun around in class one day and exclaimed: "Young man, that's one of the most perceptive questions I've ever been asked. Frankly, I cannot answer it now. My answer would be too superficial, but I'll think about it."

That professor's stock hit the ceiling for us students because we had some frauds who always tried to give the impression they were infallible. I think one of the problems of evangelicals is that because we are committed to the truth we think we have to have all the answers. Nobody has all the answers. (Some of us don't even know the right questions.)

I think our Lord's encounter with the woman of Samaria was a masterpiece of communication. How would you like the task of confronting a woman with the fact that she's had five husbands? And, furthermore, the one she's living with is not her husband? Where did Jesus begin? He doesn't say, "Lady, your first problem is a moral one." He begins by asking her for a drink. That's why she came—to get water. That starts a dialogue which slides right into the moral and spiritual problems. By a series of graduated steps in communication, Jesus got to the heart of the matter—and of the woman. And she quickly became a witness to others.

PREPARE WELL

Jesus didn't have to prepare His talks ahead of time, but we do. If we don't "sweat" in preparation, our listeners have to make up for our lapse. This is the way we often lose listeners: we haven't prepared ourselves to speak clearly, directly, and concisely.

I've heard a person make five statements which could have been incorporated in one good statement if he had known how to speak effectively. In speech as well as in meat cutting, we trim away the fat and get rid of superfluous material. Make everything contribute to your purpose. Clarification and simplification take work and more work.

Preparation has many facets. Did you ever consider that you might not be getting through because of poor enunciation, for example? That's not as unlikely as it may sound. In some situations you have to stress clear enunciation to overcome distractions. Or you may have a slight case of hoof-in-mouth disease!

When I first went to college, I enrolled for private music lessons. I'll never forget the teacher, Mrs. Mackenzie. At the end of a lesson she would give me an assignment, and she would usually say, "Now, Howie, I want you to take this and read it over and . . . (mumble, blur, fog)."

"I beg your pardon," I inquired.

And her next words would clear it up a bit. She did this every week to me till I finally caught on: she was talking to me the way I was speaking to her. I thought, *Good night! Do I talk like that?* So I went around the campus, saying carefully, "I-am-Howie-Hendricks. Do-you-understand-what-I-am-saying?"

My friends would say, "Yes—for the first time."

If a person has nothing to say, I don't care if I don't hear. But if he is speaking the truth of God, I want to hear every word he has to say. And that's the speaker's responsibility.

A columnist for the *Dallas Morning News* heard a group of little kids singing, "While shepherds washed their socks by night . . ." It has diluted that carol for me ever since. But a lot worse misunderstandings than that come from poor enunciation.

PREPARE BY EXPERIMENTING, OBSERVING, EVALUATING

I suggest you try new ways of communicating—experiment in new approaches and methods. There is no perfect way for everyone and every situation. The best method is a variety of methods. Also, study the methods of effective communicators. Ask them questions if you can; read books; do anything to become more effective in this art. This is a developed skill; it takes time.

Every communicator—every witness—should check up regularly

on himself to evaluate his communication. At the seminary I write a critique of each class I teach as soon after the class as possible. I can't evaluate perfectly how I came across, but student reactions and my own experience give me many indicators which have made a difference for subsequent classes. Sometimes you can get direct feedback. It's practice and repetition that give us mortals hope for a little perfection.

I remember a student whose wife was especially sharp. She had a master's degree, and her questions in a wives' class at the seminary were extremely perceptive. She went with her husband on preaching assignments, and at that time he had only one sermon with several variations. After his wife heard it the fifth time, she said to him, "You know, Honey, I'm just beginning to understand what you've been talking about!"

You can imagine this evaluation marked a milepost in this young man's learning process! He wasn't likely to expect every pearl of wisdom he uttered to be understood and treasured by his hearers—especially with the first exposure.

TOO MUCH TROUBLE

All these efforts to learn how to communicate better may seem far beyond what should be expected of an "ordinary" Christian. But no Christian is "ordinary"; he is a person who has been commanded by his Master to "go into all the world and preach [tell] the Gospel to every creature."

Learning to communicate the Gospel is also learning to live abundantly.

Christians have the only message that can change the world. If you're truly following Jesus Christ, this message grips you, you're continually thinking more clearly about it, feeling more deeply with people, and acting more consistently so your words are reinforced by your life.

The growing Christian is the communicating Christian.

"SELLING" THE PROSPECT

Chapter Five

A communicator is a salesman of concepts. His commodity is a message, and a Christian communicator has to "sell" his product to the prospect, though the product—salvation—is actually a gift. One of the salesman's best assets is enthusiasm—the exuberance of a satisfied owner.

Suppose I were to stop by your home to introduce you to my new tree-trimming service. You answer the door and I ask, "You don't have any trees that need trimming, do you?"

"Yes, as a matter of fact I do," you reply.

"Oh, really?" I sound surprised and uncertain.

"Could you give me an estimate?" you ask.

"I guess I can," I say slowly. "I usually just start and see how it looks, and then how long it takes, and, go from there. . . ."

How many trees do you think I would trim with such tactics? About as many as the number of people I'd win for Christ with the same approach. If the average Christian were paid on the basis of his communicative skill, he might starve to death. How do we know if we're communicating the truth of God? By how many people "buy the product."

Many people connect enthusiasm with noise, but it has no connection whatever. An enthusiastic person is one who feels very deeply and excitedly about something. He's not the person who gives what I call the three-buckets-of-ashes-on-Main-Street talk—that is, gobbledygook. Conversely, he's the person who says, "You've gotta hear this. . . . You don't understand it? . . . Let's go over it again. . . . Let's say it another way. . . . This is the best thing you've ever heard. . . ."

You know, I don't spend five minutes with Bill Bright without getting excited. After a long session with him recently, I know that he is thoroughly convinced Christians will reach the entire world with the Gospel by 2000. That's not a nice slogan for Campus Crusade; that is exactly what he believes. If Campus Crusade does not reach the world by 2000 I believe they will get further in doing it than the rest of us put together for the simple reason that this goal grips them. I have spoken to thousands of trainees and staff members of this organization from all over the world, and at the end they stood and hollered: "Right on!" It is obvious these Christians are dealing with more than a nice set of ideas!

GET EXCITED

I tell my students—reverently—that we've got to *be excited for God's sake*. And if we want somebody else to bleed, we're going to have to hemorrhage—spiritually speaking.

Enthusiasm isn't everything, of course, but it is a *sine qua non*, and it can come in small unadorned packages as well as splashy ones. This was vividly illustrated to me at a Sunday School convention in Moody Church in Chicago.

A number of us who were speaking there went across the street to get a hamburger. The place was crowded and people were standing in line. An elderly lady was in front of me. I guessed she was about 65—she was 83, I learned later. She wore a convention badge, so I knew she was a conferee. There was a table for four open, so two friends and I invited her to join us.

I asked her the obvious question, "Do you teach a Sunday School class?"

"Oh, I certainly do," she said.

I visualized a class of senior citizens, but asked her: "What age group do you teach?"

"I teach a class of junior-high boys."

"Junior-high boys! How many boys do you have?"

"Thirteen," she said sweetly.

"Tremendous! I suppose you come from a rather large church."

"No, sir, it's very small," she said. "We have about fifty-five in Sunday School."

Hardly daring to go on, I said, "What brings you to this Sunday School convention?"

"I'm on a pension—my husband died a number of years ago," she replied, "and, frankly, this is the first time a convention has come close enough to my home so I could afford to attend. I bought a Greyhound ticket and rode all last night to get here this morning and attend two workshops. I want to learn something that will make me a better teacher."

Three convention speakers slithered across the ground back to the convention after that encounter. I couldn't help thinking about all the frauds across America who would be breaking their arms patting themselves on the back if they had thirteen boys in a Sunday School of fifty-five. "Who, me go to a Sunday School convention? Man, I can tell *them* how to do it!" Not this woman.

You know, she tipped her hand—she told us she had a passion to communicate! I heard a sequel to this story some time later. A doctor told me there are eighty-four young men in or moving toward the Christian ministry as a result of this woman's influence! We have some in our seminary. I asked two of them, "What do you remember most about her?"

They said, "She is the most unforgettable person we've ever met. She's still going hard—fills her car with kids and brings them to church."

Show me a person with a passion to communicate, and I'll show you a person who will learn how to get the job done. He'll read books, pick everybody's brains, go to any kind of training session to find out how to improve. Some of the most brilliant individuals I know show up at conferences, and I'm tempted to say, "Friend, what in the world are you doing here?"

They'll look me straight in the eye and say, "Brother, I came to learn, and I'm going to drink till I'm full!"

But how does one get and maintain this holy enthusiasm? It's a spiritual problem; there are no two ways about it.

People have asked me: "How do you get so excited about teaching the same subjects after thirty-nine years of it?" I'll clue you, it's not always easy. But something that helps is getting alone with the Lord before class. He and I have some fascinating conversations. Sometimes it's almost an argument, because I'm very human and my clay feet can't be concealed just by wearing shoes. Sometimes I get tired and discouraged and feeling sorry for myself. In the process of talking with the Lord, He reminds me every time: "Hendricks, your primary problem is spiritual; you're hung up on Hendricks."

That office rug, not the classroom, is my battleground. Before class I get freshly charged for my mission. I realize anew that though I've said it a thousand times, these students have never heard it, and they've got to hear it. I pour on the "gasoline" there, and the Lord ignites me!

BE YOURSELF

Do you have the personality of a salesman? If not, it just may be that the Lord will give you one. Personality is important because you communicate by what you are. Your personality becomes the lens through which the Spirit focuses His truth, and no matter how clear or obscure your message, your personality shines through.

Would you believe that God doesn't want you to be another Vonette Bright or Billy Graham, but to be yourself? You are different from anyone else, and you are most attractive when you are yourself, simply because real is attractive. And you are least attractive when you're trying to be like somebody else.

Do you know which bones are the smallest in the human body? There are three of them, and they are located in your middle ear. The average medical student finds them only with difficulty: the malleus, incus, and the stapes. You hear through these three bones only when they are in proper functioning order.

One of the most exciting surgeries I have ever witnessed is what is called a stapedectomy. It's an operation performed on the third smallest of these bones. I watched a man operated on who had not heard anything in twenty-six years. The patient was under partial anesthesia, and as the surgeon was about to join the bones, he said, "Howie, keep talking as I join the bones, and keep your eyes glued to his eyes."

The instant the surgeon joined those bones, the man's eyes got like saucers. He said, "W-w-what's that? Who's talking?"

"Why," he said, "that's me! That's *my* voice I hear!" Tears streamed down the man's face, and a nurse wiped them away with some gauze.

You know, in the body of Christ, size does not determine the significance of the members. A Christian may belittle himself because he's not an "arm." But he may be as a "stapes" for clearly transmitting communications, and he is an essential part of the body.

We need to allow the Holy Spirit to pour His transforming truth through our personalities and channel the overflow to others. Don't forget that the Spirit used some forty different authors to pen the inspired Scriptures. He poured the Father's message through the life of each of these men, and it took on their mark for the purpose God intended. He will do the same sort of thing in us.

LEARN TO LISTEN
It's so easy for us to have a superficial contact with people—and

consequently superficial communication. You have a gift to offer—a product to "sell"—but you may not sense the silent plea of the "customer." This comes across when you're able to listen with interest and concern.

One of our seminary students learned the hard way. He was counseling with a woman who had an involved problem. She kept going on with the story, and it was getting late in a long afternoon. He had said wearily, "Yes, Madam, and what else happened?" Suddenly, in the middle of a sentence, she got up and walked out the door. As she was vanishing, he blurted, "Oh, are you through?"

"No, you are," she called back. They both were.

One of the great needs we have if we are to become a significant person for Jesus Christ is to learn how to listen. It's an extremely difficult art. You must be able to cut off all else in the environment and concentrate totally on what's in front of you.

Perhaps you have been talking to a person and suddenly you sense he's wandering away mentally. He catches himself and looks back at you, but the situation appears hopeless—and maybe it is. This person may be still vibrating from a knockdown battle with his spouse that morning. Or perhaps a business deal is gnawing inside. Whatever the problem is, it would be better to stop and ask, "Friend, is there something bothering you? Can I do anything?"

If a person is really hurting, you aren't going to get through to him by sheer enthusiasm. When I encounter a person in this condition, I give him a chance to talk. It shows I'm interested in him as a person, and I may get a chance to really help.

OTHER OBSTACLES TO "SALES"

There's another kind of resistance expected by experienced salesmen. It's natural, because the average person goes through three stages in the process of embracing an idea. First of all, he tends to resist it. His defenses go up the moment you hit him with something new. The second step—if you reach it—is toleration. The third—our goal—is acceptance. The Christian witness works on the art of the first and second steps—and prays for the joy of the Holy Spirit's accomplishment of the third.

Lack of time will always be one of the problems in communication. It's one of the great stresses of the century—how to make time for communicating with people. And the more renowned you become in our society, usually the greater this problem is.

A young man at Texas Tech University told me, "Prof, I sure wish it were like five years ago when nobody knew me. I was just a zero when I landed on campus, and then this most exciting ministry developed." Now he spends most of his time engineering the big program, and he has little time for people. That's sad.

The press of time makes more critical the need for busy Christian workers to get alone with God and their Bibles for spiritual renewal. Bending your knees and opening the Book helps put time into proper perspective with eternity.

Salesmen must have self-confidence. This may be their most outstanding characteristic. Most of us have trouble building confidence. Surprisingly, this is a problem with some of our seminary students. All of them are graduates from colleges or universities, all have a B or above average, all have highest references, and as far as we can determine, they have a gift of speaking. One nearly bowled me over when he said, "Prof, I'm thinking of bailing out."

When I recovered enough to ask why, he said, "Frankly, I just don't think I can cut it in the ministry." I thought to myself, *If you don't have it, no one does!* But that's how he felt until he became gripped with the reality that, as a Christian, he is a significant person with a spiritual gift to employ.

The wonderful possibility for Christian "salesmen" is to develop a complete Christ-confidence. This is not cockiness but a confidence and reliance in Christ. The fruit of the Spirit is self-control—that is, control of self by the Holy Spirit within you. This goes as far beyond self-confidence as sunlight beyond a sunlamp. When the Holy Spirit is vitally involved, we extend the gift of life to people with enthusiasm and confidence.

TRAINING COMMUNICATORS

Chapter Six

I'll never forget hearing Douglas Hyde the ex-Communist turned Roman Catholic. He said when he first came into the Communist Party he was thrilled by its basic principles. The first one was that everyone is a potential communicator of Communism. That was exciting, but his first assignment almost disillusioned him.

Hyde went to a factory to address a group of workers, and when he was through everybody walked out except one man who came up and said, "C-c-c-c-c-can I b-b-b-become a C-c-c-communist?"

Hyde froze with embarrassment, and the inquirer stumbled through the plea again. Hyde blurted: "Come back and talk to me next week."

At Hyde's cell group meeting, his superiors berated him. "You are an unbeliever. There's no exception to the 'potential principle.' You sign that man up."

Hyde went back to the same group, and the same applicant came. "C-c-c-c-can I b-b-b-b-become a C-c-c-c-communist?" he repeated. Now he was welcomed and in time became a high-ranking member of the Communist Party in charge of their literature program around the world.

Is every Christian a potential communicator of Jesus Christ? Certainly, but he needs training. There are no naturally perfect communicators—except Jesus, who was perfect in every way.

There aren't many significant books on the subject of Jesus' training of His disciples, but I recommend several which can be read with extreme profit. The first is the classic *The Training of the Twelve*, by A.B. Bruce. This is a masterpiece of exegetical work with profound implications for disciple-building. A section dealing with Christ's choice of the disciples is worth the price of the book. This is a book to be studied; I have read it many times and have profited each time.

Another book is *Teaching Techniques of Jesus*, by Herman H. Horne, who was for many years the distinguished professor of education at New York University. He was a contemporary with humanist John Dewey, but Horne was committed to a Christian position. This is an excellent guide into firsthand study of the Scriptures. The thing I like most about Horne is that he raises more questions than he answers.

More recently, Robert Coleman has contributed several significant books, the most famous of which is *The Master Plan of Evangelism*.

For those interested in further training materials on the subject, contact Search Ministries of Lutherville, Maryland.

EXAMPLE STIMULATES INQUIRY

What were the means Christ used in training men? He taught by *example*, and His disciples observed Him intimately, discriminatingly. One example concerns prayer.

When I received Christ as my Saviour at age nine at an evangelistic meeting, I went with many others to a big room for the follow-up session. There a counselor lectured us on twenty-seven or so things a believer needs to know, none of which was in written form. At that point I was dazed by the realization that my sins were forgiven, and things the instructor said didn't impress me much. At the end I got up and walked out the door, supposedly prepared to live the Christian life—including praying.

It's interesting that Jesus didn't introduce the subject of prayer in this manner at all. The disciples themselves asked, "Lord, teach us to pray." This came *after* observing prayer in the life of our Lord. They constantly found that His number-one priority was fellowship with the infinite God. I believe the key to training is getting the trainee to ask the right questions, and the best way to stimulate questions is by setting the example.

Who ruins the curiosity God built into mankind? Often it is the most significant people in a person's life: his parents and his teachers. The child keeps asking questions, and the adults keep saying, "Be quiet," or, "How should I know?"

I often ask Sunday School teachers which child they like the best in their classes, and usually it's the one who seldom opens his mouth. He sits there with a big grin and twenty years later is still sitting around. By the time students get to seminary, it's quite a process for us to resurrect that curiosity factor so God can educate them.

In Philippians 4:9 we see Paul as an example for young Christians. He says, "Those things that you have both learned and received and heard, and seen in me, do." Paul's students had a sort of audiovisual presentation, and they actively learned.

The first time I really noticed Paul's words: "Follow me as I follow Christ," I thought, *How egotistical can you get!* But the longer I think about it the more impressed I am by the fact that *whether one says that or not, the leader is being followed.* The question leaders have to ask is, "Am I following Christ?"

Jesus Christ was the perfect Man, so He had no failures to share. But I believe the good human trainer can be so secure in Christ that he is able to share his failures with trainees. This information can be instructive and actually encouraging to beginners.

Some leaders try to project an image of wisdom and strength, which is misleading as well as harmful. I think this is a major reason why many people in our churches will not come to their pastors for consultation before situations become desperate. A person with a problem is reluctant to approach a plaster saint who wouldn't understand. Young Christians need to know that they aren't alone in feeling inadequate.

PARTICIPATION IS PREREQUISITE TO LEARNING

The second means that our Lord used was *participation*. Mark 3:14 says: "He ordained twelve that they should be with Him and that He might send them forth to preach." The key to the training ministry of Jesus Christ is that He participated with them in the ministry. He shared His life. Occasionally He was alone, and sometimes they worked without Him, but most of the time the Lord was with His disciples. In the midst of their experiences, they asked the majority of their questions, so the teaching and experience were inseparably related. This makes me think training is better *caught* than taught.

Mark 4:35 introduces a choice case. Jesus had been talking about faith, comparing it to a mustard seed. Wow! How would you like to listen to Jesus Christ discuss the subject of faith? Well, after He gets to the end of this, He gives them an "exam"—but not like the ones we give at school.

He says, "Gentlemen, the lectures are over; let's go to the other side of the lake." And into the boat they go.

But when they get in the middle of the lake, they've got problems—a sudden storm overwhelms them and they're sinking! (Mind you, these were not seminary students; these were professional fishermen.) And they scream, "Lord, don't You even care?"

So Jesus rebukes the wind; no problem there. And then He turns to the disciples and says, "How is it that *you*, of all people, have no faith?" They had just heard the lesson, the lecture. But people don't learn faith through lectures; they learn it through living. And the disciples got a big, fat F on this exam!

I have come to believe that tension is essential as an ingredient to growth. I don't mean anxiety; I mean outside pressure and stress. The early Christians got moving when they were catapulted by the persecution out of their safe situation in Jerusalem. I think we need to get our people moving by stirring up the nest. We are often so comfortable that we're vulnerable to the evil one's anesthetic.

A student met me on the campus some time ago and said, "Hey, Prof, I'm going out to SMU—one of those fraternity Bible studies."

"Oh," I said. "Wonderful!"

"Will you pray for me?" he asked.

"I sure will," I answered.

"I kinda think you're not praying for me the way I think I need," he said slowly.

"How's that?"

"Well, I could wish that you would pray that these guys would not go for my throat."

"Friend, I'm coming through loud and clear," I told him. "I'm going to pray that they'll go right for your jugular vein—that they'll nail you to the wall!"

The next morning I met him on the campus and said, "How did you make out?"

"The Lord answered your prayers," he said ruefully.

You know, that student is a prime prospect for training! He *knows* what he doesn't know, and that's a lot better position than many of us are in.

In his booklet, *Dedication and Leadership,* Douglas Hyde, the ex-Communist, tells how these all-out atheists train their recruits. A new member is sent to infect a group with the Red philosophy. They decimate him, and he comes back reeling. "How did it go?" he's asked.

"Oh, terrible."

"Great," they say.

"Do you have something else that will help me?"

"Right. Sit down."

They give him the second lesson and send him out. He gets knocked down again, and his teachers set him up for lesson three.

How do we Christians do it? We fill Christians' minds till it's coming out their ears, and they get so spiritually obese they can hardly move. Some of them eventually get fed up and quietly drop out.

I like to drop my students into a juvenile home in Dallas for experience in counseling. I don't care if they can memorize and repeat what they hear in class. What I want to know is whether they can communicate when I deposit them in a room out there with juvenile delinquents. If they can't, I haven't trained them sufficiently.

PERSONAL INVOLVEMENT PRODUCES INTEREST

Third, Christ taught by *personalized instruction*. In Luke 9:18 and following, Jesus is recorded as asking: "Whom do men say that I am?" And they shot out the answers they had picked up in the streets. "But whom say *ye* that I am?" Jesus persisted. Peter responded with the revelation God had given him, and now the disciples are strongly and personally involved.

I have found that the closer I get to an individual, the more influence I have on his life. I *talk* to many students; unfortunately I *teach* very few. Those I teach, I change, and that requires personal involvement. Sometimes while students are filing out of class I say: "Come out to my house tonight."

"What are you going to do, Prof?"

"I don't know; come on out."

So eight or ten guests come out to the house and we sit around sipping Cokes as we talk. And before we know it, it's 2:30 in the morning—and nobody is saying, "When's the period over, Prof?" And long after they've forgotten the classroom, they're still moving as a result of what they picked up through personalized instruction.

I saw a friend's wife in the church parking lot some time ago and she said, "What in the world are you doing to my husband?"

"Why, what's the matter with him?" I asked.

"I have to set the alarm clock to tell this guy to put down his Bible and go to bed at night."

And when I return from a trip, it's likely my wife will tell me: "Telephone call from——." And he will have a list of questions to fire at me. He's involved because I got involved with him.

REBUKE MAY BE NECESSARY

Most of us miss something in training that is very valuable. Christ used it throughout the Gospels—carefully. I'm talking about *rebuke*. He did not rebuke them because they were not using the right methods but for lack of faith.

A man in Wheaton, Illinois changed the whole course of my life when I was a student at Wheaton College. He called me into his office, sat me down, and every time I opened my mouth he said, "Keep your mouth shut and listen." I came out of that office so mad I could have spit nails. But today I call this man blessed because he's the only man who cared enough about me to face me with hard facts about my stubborn self-will. I made a 180-degree turn that I'm still following.

"Open rebuke is better than hidden love! Wounds from a friend are better than kisses from an enemy!" (Prov. 27:5-6, TLB)

We say we don't want to hurt anybody, but we're hurting them in droves by refusing to do necessary surgery. Some time ago I went to my doctor with some physical problems, and he took some pictures of the premises. After examining them, he said, "Hendricks, you've got a rock collection down there. Since you're not a geologist, we'll have to take them out." Would you believe it, this friend had me sliced up and he never shed a tear. He knew he had to hurt me in order to heal me.

How many people have gone off the road because some of us do not love them enough to face them with the facts of life? We should examine this aspect of ministry the Lord might give to us.

DELEGATING RESPONSIBILITY ENERGIZES WORKERS

Then, by actually *delegating the Great Commission* to the disciples, Jesus further trained them. I have never gotten over this in Mark 16:14-15. "Afterward He appeared unto the eleven as they sat at meat, and upbraided them with their unbelief and hardness of heart, because they believed not those who had seen Him after He was risen. And He said unto them: Go ye into all the world."

I could understand if Jesus gave the Great Commission to graduates of the finest schools—but when I look at that group of ragtag disciples who fled from the cross and retreated to hideaways, I marvel that Jesus bothered with them.

Yet this illuminates a basic fact of training: you train a man in proportion to the confidence you have in him. Jesus knew what these men would accomplish after they were filled with His Spirit. We often give up too soon on trainees and fail to invest ourselves in them.

We had a boy in our seminary a few years ago whom I misjudged completely. I figured he was sleeping through many of our classes and that he would never make it in vocational Christian work. He did manage to graduate, however, and took a church in Canada. Eighteen pastors in a row had walked away from it as a hopeless situation. When I heard our graduate had accepted it, I thought: *That's par for the course; the poor boy doesn't even know enough not to take it.* Some time later we began to get reports of small miracles up there. I couldn't believe it, but I got a chance to visit there and was invited to speak.

People were hanging out the doors when I arrived. It was so crowded I had to give my chair to a man on the platform so he could sit down while I was preaching. After 127 years, they were having their first building program!

An oculist friend of mine in Dallas was active in his church for many years but was doing no witnessing. One day someone from Campus Crusade for Christ said to him, "Doctor, are you sharing your faith?"

"No. To be honest with you, I don't know how."

Campus Crusade had a training institute coming, so he was enrolled. He learned the Four Spiritual Laws and how to share them with other people. As part of a team, he went out to Love Field, where he witnessed to people and saw them trust Christ as Saviour. He got so turned on he thought he should use this in his profession.

My friend started putting the Four Laws booklets in his waiting room beside the magazines. Later he projected the Four Spiritual Laws on the wall for his patrons to read instead of the meaningless letters that you try to read when you visit other oculists. This man has led more people to Christ in the city of Dallas than anyone else I know, minister or lay person.

I was in a section of India and told this story in a conference without mentioning the doctor's name. Afterward an Indian doctor came up and said, "You were talking about Dr. _____ , weren't you?"

"Yeah; how did you know?"

"I went to the university in Dallas for graduate work," he said, "and my eyes went bad on me."

"I get the picture," I told him.

And now in that part of India, the only qualified professional in his field is having a consistent witness for Jesus Christ because a doctor in Dallas learned to witness.

INDIVIDUAL BIBLE STUDY IS INDISPENSABLE

Shortly after I became a Christian, I said to a man who told me to get into the Word, "Fine. Where shall I begin?"

He said, "Hendricks, it doesn't make any difference. It's all inspired."

So I went home and got a Bible out and landed in Ezekiel—right in the midst of the "wheels." I read a while, and I thought this must be an exception to the "inspired" rule, so I turned to the back of the Bible and landed in Revelation—right in the midst of the bowls and the vials and the wraths. I'm ashamed to say that the Bible was a closed Book to me for one solid year after that, and I was convinced that the Roman Catholic Church was right in teaching that we need professional help to interpret the Bible.

About a year later a man asked me if I was studying the Bible for myself. I told him I wasn't, and he asked the reason. "Well, I tried it once."

He said, "Howie, will you meet with me once a week? I'll teach you how to get into it."

Every week we got together, and he gave me a couple of things to look for. Like a little kid with a new fire engine, I'd dig into the passage and ransack it to find the answers to those two or three questions. Then I'd run back and unload all of my pearls on him. He got excited, and that turned me on more. That continued for some time until I was studying daily on my own.

I am personally committed to teaching people how to get into the Bible for themselves. This is essential. We have a lot of people under the teaching of the Word, but not in it for themselves. It's exciting to start a young person on a process that will never end. And if he should go to India or to Africa and the boat goes down with all his study notes, all he needs to get back into action is to go to a bookstore and buy another Bible.

At the conclusion of the Dallas Cowboy football training camp one summer, a young man who had joined the team came to my office and we built a friendship. He was a Christian but he was floundering. I asked him if he was in the Word on a regular basis, and he said no. I asked if he'd like to meet with me, and so we started. Before long God placed on this young man's heart the burden of starting a camping program for young people. He came hurrying into my office one day and announced, "Well, I did it."

I asked him what he'd done.

He said, "I just mortgaged my home. If we're going to get this thing off the ground, I've got to have some bucks to back it up." How many Christians do you know who are willing to mortgage their home for Christ? And that's not the end of the story.

After he got his camp started, Hurricane Carla came along and wiped it out! With a pilot friend I flew over to the camp to offer some comfort, and when we arrived, we found this hulking gridder and his wife standing in the middle of the rubble, singing: "To God be the glory, great things He hath done!" Is it any wonder that I rank personal Bible study at the top of requirements for Christian growth?

We have barely scratched the surface in examining principles of training communicators. If you want to dig deeper, in addition to studying the three books mentioned earlier in this chapter, I suggest you search the four Gospels with the following questions in mind:

1. How did God launch the church?

An infinite God might have used an infinite number of means. The real question is why He used the means He did. Would you have chosen the twelve men whom Christ chose? I would not. I don't think there is a businessman in America who would have selected the men Jesus did in order to launch a worldwide enterprise. This tells me that we haven't learned very well how to select promising leaders.

2. What controlled Christ's use of His time?

Where and how did He spend it? He had only three and a half years to carry out His mission, and at the end He could say, "I have finished the work!"

3. What was uppermost in the mind of Christ while training the Twelve?

What were His objectives? His priorities? Is His value system revealed in His training program?

4. Why don't the Gospels contain only the words and works of Christ?

Why include such inane comments as Peter's statement on the Mount of Transfiguration: "Lord, it's good to be here"? And why so many reports of failure?

5. Why was it good strategy to forsake to a degree His public ministry to concentrate on training twelve men?

6. How prominent and important are the disciples in the various events—in places they are not mentioned, are we to assume they were not present?

7. Why did men follow Christ?

Was it because of His personality? Did they follow Him because of the signs? How do we explain the fact that the greatest teacher of all had casualties?

When you have answered these questions from the Gospels, you are well on the road toward determining what is involved in disciple-building.

Training communicators is a demanding yet delicate process. But Christian teachers are never alone in it. When God steps into the training situation, we discover the full dimension of the process. Marvelous things begin to happen, and you realize that you as the trainer didn't do much except be available as God's instrument for the accomplishment of His will.

LIVING THE MESSAGE

Part 3

WITH GOD

Chapter Seven

To me personally, one of the most convicting verses in the New Testament is in 1 Corinthians 9. A number of years ago the Spirit of God used it to place a burr under my spiritual saddle, and I have been scratching ever since. "In a race, everyone runs, but only one person gets first prize. So run your race to win" (v. 24, TLB).

The passage continues: "To win the contest you must deny yourself many things that would keep you from doing your best. An athlete goes to all this trouble just to win a blue ribbon or a silver cup, but we do it for a heavenly reward that never disappears. So I run straight to the goal with purpose in every step. I fight to win. I'm not just shadowboxing or playing around. Like an athlete I punish my body, treating it roughly, training it to do what it should, not what it wants to. Otherwise I fear that after enlisting others for the race, I myself might be declared unfit and ordered to stand aside" (1 Cor. 9:25-27, TLB).

If this peril was a possibility to the Apostle Paul, what must it be to us—the chance of being approved by men but disqualified by God? This may be why Paul said to Timothy, "Do your utmost to present yourself to God approved, a workman who has no cause to be ashamed, correctly analyzing the message of the truth" (2 Tim. 2:15, MLB). A Christian communicator must maintain a vital relationship with God to establish fruitful relationships with people, and certain factors are indispensable for this.

Know the Word

The first is a *daily intake of the Word of God.* As a second-year student at Dallas Theological Seminary, I heard Dr. L.S. Chafer say: "Gentlemen, don't study for a class; study for a lifetime of ministry."

Any student knows that his first task in academia is to read between the teacher's sentences—find out what it takes to survive under each professor. To study for a lifetime of ministry had never occurred to me. His words launched a program for me that I have continued to this day. I set aside one hour every day for personal study of the Word of God—not in commentaries or secondary sources, but the Bible itself. This is in addition to other study I do for preaching and teaching. Such study has become the reservoir out of which I have been privileged to minister.

In Acts 8 we have the thrilling story of Philip's ministry in Samaria, then to the Ethiopian official. The Spirit of God told Philip to leave Samaria and go on a wilderness mission. Had it been me, I would have said, "Lord, I'm involved in a citywide crusade, remember? My gift is not this one-to-one stuff. I'm a metropolitan man!" But Philip ran to intercept the African's chariot in the wilderness, and he found the traveler reading the Scripture as he bounced along. Philip knew his mission: "Do you understand what you are reading?" he asked. Then Philip "began at the same Scripture, and preached unto him Jesus," the text says (Acts 8:35).

If someone were reading Deuteronomy 27, could you start with him there and explain Jesus on the basis of the Old Testament? This requires a knowledge of the Old Testament. When the need arose, Philip had the goods—he was able to deliver and communicate God's truth.

You may be sharing Christ with others, but are *you* growing? Are you feeding yourself on a daily ingestion of the truth of God's Word? Are you being ministered to as you minister? I spend my life ministering the Word of God at the seminary and out across the country, but I dry up spiritually unless I have the ministry of the Spirit through His Word every day. We communicate out of a transformed life—not out of a vacuum. This calls for much more than casual reading or superficial study of the Word.

One of the men who made a great impact on my life was Dr. Donald Grey Barnhouse, late pastor of Tenth Presbyterian Church, Philadelphia. I was associated with him for a number of years, working with college students. One day I asked him a question that I almost wished afterward I hadn't. I said, "Dr. Barnhouse, what do you suggest would enable me to communicate as effectively as you do?"

He whipped around as if I had hit him with a lash and said, "Hendricks, are you willing to pay the price I pay to communicate God's truth?" He told me about traveling on a train one day and sitting across from a seminary student reading *Time* magazine while Dr. Barnhouse was reading the Book of Romans. The student recognized Dr. Barnhouse and engaged him in conversation, then asked him essentially the same question I had. Dr. Barnhouse told him: "Son, as long as you continue to read that magazine more than you do this Book, you will know more about that than you will about this."

You see, there's a premium on communication—a high one that calls for a great deal of sacrifice.

There's more to the doctrine of salvation than the Four Spiritual Laws or any other clear plan of salvation. You can go a long way with the Four Laws, but don't ever stop there. There's a lot more to the doctrine of Christian experience than the filling of the Spirit; don't stop there. You want to continue to be simple in your presentation of the Gospel, but in order to be a better communicator even at the simple level you need to know more than the basics.

Wouldn't it be a circus if we dressed according to our spiritual maturity? How many people would we see—saved for many years—toddling around the church in diapers, still waving their rattles, cooing, exploring their newly discovered toes?

I served in a church where an elder repeatedly testified: "Thirty-seven years ago the Lord saved me. 'The Lord is my Shepherd, I shall not want,'" and then he sat down. In testimony meetings some early adolescent would get up and quote Psalm 23:1 while this elder was preparing to play his record, and you could almost see the elder think, *Good night, there goes my verse,* as he sank back in the pew. I always thought, *You'd think in thirty-seven years he'd learn a second verse just in case he got caught in this predicament!*

The most exciting thing about the Christian life is that it's an adventure that never ends. There is a true sense in which we are pursuing flying goals. A seminary student will often raise a scriptural question and ask: "Prof, would you explain this?"

"I can't explain that," I'll answer.

"You mean you don't know anything about it?"

"Oh, I know something about it, and I'll tell you what I know, but that doesn't explain it."

"Really? You mean you can't *explain* it?"

"No, I can't. Does that really bother you? It would bother me as a finite person if I *could* fully comprehend an Infinite Mind. The fact that God has revealed Himself and invited me into the fascinating process of gaining ever-increasing insight into His revelation is the thing that drives me onward. Never stop studying the message—get a tighter grip on the truth and let truth get a vise grip on you, and God will give you light."

HOME LIFE IS CRUCIAL

A second survival factor for Christian growth is *keeping up on your "homework"*—run that by again: homework—*work at home.* Your home life cannot be separated from your ministry. This is the thrust of Paul's argument in his first epistle to Timothy: Don't put a man in spiritual leadership until his home life passes examination. For if a man doesn't know how to rule his own home, how can he rule in the house of God? (See 1 Tim. 3:4-5.) The home is the personal proving grounds for a public ministry. (See chapters 8 and 9, this book.) Show me a man who keeps a cutting edge in public, and I will show you a man who keeps a cutting edge in private. Many a man tries to use his public ministry as a cover for failing in the basic responsibility God has given him at home. Sooner or later, he is almost certain to face incredible dissonance.

I have a pastor friend with four children. He has served Jesus Christ for thirty-two years in a effective ministry. He's been a soul-winner, a disciple-builder, and he has fed a steady stream of young men into the ministry. But by his own testimony he has lost his own four children. One is in a penitentiary; another is on drugs; one of his girls has been unhappily married three times; and the other daughter has a scandalous moral reputation. Weeping as I have seldom seen a man weep, he said to me, "I've lost my confidence and self-respect. How can I tell others what Jesus Christ can do in their lives when I never allowed Him to work in my own home?"

KEEP LEARNING

A third survival factor is *stretch your intellectual muscles*. The mind is like a muscle; it develops from usage, but you have to be very careful what you feed it. I can tell a lot about a man by what he reads. If you feed your mind on garbage-pail literature, you're going to develop a garbage-pail mentality. Beyond this, there is a great deal in print that will never stretch your mind or soul.

I suggest every Christian undertake a worthwhile reading program. Paul directed Christians to think about things that are true, honorable, just, pure, lovely, and praiseworthy because these things edify us and develop us as servants of Christ. (See Phil. 4:8.) Good books can supply rich food for thought. You should be exposed to significant people and their ideas—and you can experience this through reading.

In this larger contact you enrich your understanding and ability to communicate the Scriptures. Hardening of the personal viewpoint is far more lethal than hardening of the arteries. This has nothing to do with your age; it has everything to do with your attitude. I have friends who are eighty-four and are dynamic in their growth. I have students of twenty-four who are dead in the head—and everywhere else!

I saw a cartoon epitaph not long ago that was beautiful: "Died aged twenty-seven—buried aged sixty-four." It's amazing how many dead people are running around loose. Caleb at eighty years of age asked God: "Give me that mountain." He wasn't ready for retirement; he wanted to conquer the most difficult place for God!

Some time ago an airliner I was slated to take was oversold on coach reservations, so they asked if I'd mind riding first class. I love such options, and I sat down next to a man who I soon discovered was Charlton Heston, the famous actor who played Moses in *The Ten Commandments*. (He didn't recognize me right away, but we still had a good talk.) I have learned to keep my mouth shut when around great people except to ask questions, and I plied Heston with questions. Finally I said, "Mr. Heston, what in your judgment is the secret to your communication skill?"

He turned to me and with that magnificent voice said, "Sir, I have never gotten over the miracle that someone would come to listen to me speak."

That sort of stunned me. I'm concerned about *my* drawing a crowd, and Charlton Heston marvels that people come to hear him. I'm convinced that a man's commitment to his message is measured by the significance of his words when he has to speak to only a handful of people.

KNOW YOUR ADVERSARY

A fourth survival requirement is: *know your enemy.* Reading in Luke, I was intrigued by the interesting expression with which Jesus' temptation account begins: "And Jesus . . . was led by the

Spirit into the wilderness" (Luke 4:1, KJV). This was no reckless exposure to Satan on the part of Jesus. Our Saviour never underestimated the enemy—so how can I afford to?

Paul said, "Let him that thinketh he standeth take heed lest he fall" (1 Cor. 10:12). At the very point in which you think you're strong—that's where you are vulnerable.

I was talking to a group of students some time ago, and I warned that living in a cesspool society such as we do means that Satan will bait traps with sexual sin. A student came up afterward and said, "I appreciate that, Prof, but I really think you've missed it. This is no problem to me. I got this all under control."

That was two years ago, and recently we expelled this student from the seminary for sexual promiscuity. It reminds me of Peter's claim: "Lord, You can count on me—I don't know about the rest of these guys, but I'm right with You."

Not long afterward a girl comes up to him and says, "Hey, you're one of those followers of Jesus."

"Who, me? Never heard of Him."

If you're saying some sin could never get you, you may already be on the road that Peter took.

You're about to step on a spiritual banana peel.

And instead of crawling all over the Christian brother who gets trapped, we'd better start saying to ourselves: "There go I but for the grace of God." The devil is after any person or organization that is doing a work for God, and he's got over 4,000 years of practical experience.

He might get us in a hundred ways, I suppose. He could get to us through doctrinal compromise, through division—his favorite tactic—through discouragement, through moral impurity, or through getting us to concentrate on secondary goals.

A profitable study of the strategy of Satan is found in the Book of Nehemiah. First Satan worked from outside the group, with opposition, with threat, and with violence; and that didn't get the job done. So he took a different tack. Nehemiah was doing a little pastoral calling one day, and he arrived at Shemaiah's house. "Man, Nehemiah, it's providential that you came. I got inside informa- tion—they are out for your neck and, friend, you had better take off for the temple real quick and hide there. I'll go with you, and we'll shut the doors tight."

Nehemiah wasn't impressed. "Should such a man as I flee? And who is there, that, being as I am, would go into the temple to save his life? I will not go in. . . . I perceived that God had not sent him . . . for Tobiah and Sanballat had hired him" (Neh. 6:11-12).

That's right, the enemy on the outside bribed the "believer" on the inside. I find in Ephesians that we are to endeavor to keep the unity of the Spirit in the bond of peace—not to make it, but to *keep* it. Let's not let Satan steal it away! And remember—he has a mixed bag of tricks.

KEEP LOOKING TO GOD

I believe that spiritual survival also demands a *heart sensitive and responsive to God.* It is easy to look to human programs or methods rather than to the God who is using them.

The disciples were out in the boat one night, and suddenly they were stabbed awake by a dim form coming toward them over the water. In typical fashion, Peter cried out, "Lord, if that's You, bid me come." (See Matt. 14:28.)

"Come on," called the Lord.

How would you like Peter's assignment—stepping over the side of the boat and shedding waves like raindrops? Peter was going great when all of a sudden he looked away from the Lord. Maybe Andrew warned him about a wave advancing on his starboard flank. Peter disappeared—almost. He prayed the shortest prayer in the Bible: "Lord, save me!" You can't cut any word out of that and get the same thing—and it's a good thing Peter didn't omit any of it.

The Lord reached out and pulled Peter up. I think Peter walked back to the boat this time with his eyes riveted on Jesus. He didn't fully learn that lesson, though, because in John 21 I find Jesus saying, "Peter, you're going to die violently before long." Just then John walked on the scene, and Peter protested, "But what about this man?"

The Lord said, "If I will that he continues to live until I come, what's that to you? Follow Me."

We can go down the tube faster by keeping our eyes on some other Christian than any other way I know. Jesus says to us: "You keep on following Me."

What was uppermost in the mind of Jesus Christ in the training of His disciples? I think it was their trust in Him. When I come to the Book of Hebrews and "God's Hall of Fame" in Chapter 11, I'm overwhelmed with the kind of people who rated mention there. We see former drunks in that chapter, and harlots, failures, and second-rate individuals—but they learned to live by faith.

BE A SERVANT

Another survival factor, perhaps the most neglected in the contemporary church, is the *practice of servanthood.* Leadership as such is never exalted in the Word of God. Instead, service is honored and rewarded.

In Matthew 20 we read of a mother who asked that her two sons be granted places of honor at the right and left hand of Jesus in heaven. Then Jesus pointed out that the princes of the Gentiles exercise dominion over the people, but the disciples would be different. "Whosoever will be great among you, let him be your minister. And whosoever will be chief among you, let him be your servant" (v. 26-27). The supreme pattern for this posture is Jesus Himself—"even as the Son of man came not to be ministered unto, but to minister, and to give His life a ransom for many" (v. 28).

I believe a great problem in evangelicalism today—whether in the local church, missions, seminary education, or what have you—is we have *too many* big-time operators! And *too few* servants.

I was in a lovely Christian home while holding a week of church meetings, and I was somewhat taken back the first night when the hostess said, "What would you like for breakfast?"

I said, "Ma'am, anything you serve will be fine for me."

"Well, how would you like your eggs?" she asked.

I said, "Any way you serve them will be all right."

"What time would you like to get up?" she continued.

"You just tell me what time you have breakfast, and I'll be there."

"Well, the children go to school and my husband works, so we have breakfast at 7 A.M., but we don't expect you to get up then."

"That's all right; I'll be here at 7 A.M. I'd love to enjoy the fellowship of your family."

This went on all week—"Would you like to have breakfast in your room?" And I kept trying to be like one of the family. One evening after the meeting, we were talking about the spiritual life, and this couple said, "You're the strangest person we've had in this house. We entertain Bible teachers, missionaries, and other Christian leaders, and each one of them has his own set of specifications. What is it with you?"

That night I had a hard time getting to sleep. What in the world are we Christians coming to? Who's kidding whom? At best, we are unprofitable servants—but who could tell it from our actions? Not until we pour our lives out like libation offerings to people can God be exalted among us as He deserves.

The greatest problems we're facing in our evangelical churches today are in the area of human relations, not doctrine. The greatest problem of missionaries is in getting along with other Christians. The greatest problem at seminaries and in all Christian organizations is getting people to learn how to live as Christians, to relate to one another, and to magnify one another. I think Jesus Christ trained His disciples as a group because He was training them to work in groups.

Paul gave some exhilarating instructions to Timothy—and to us. After mentioning the value of good example, reading, teaching, and spiritual gifts, Paul directs Timothy to "meditate upon these things;

give thyself wholly to them" (1 Tim. 4:15). The result, said Paul, will be visible evidence of God's power in us—evident spiritual progress.

People are watching us to see if our words are real. Our message and our lives are inseparably related, so the closeness of our walk with God will determine how effectively we communicate His message.

WITH YOUR MATE

Chapter Eight

Hundreds of times a day a judge's gavel drops to the desk and the dismal words resound: "Divorce granted." A marriage which began with delight has ended with disillusionment. What the couple thought were stars in their eyes turned out to be sand. What began with excitement and expectation has ended with bitterness and hostility.

There's another tragedy, not as heralded but just as lamentable as a legal divorce. That is the psychological divorce: a couple who continue to live together but with minimal communication. The relationship is shattered, and for all practical purposes the marriage is dead.

The joke about the silent couple who hadn't been communicating for some time isn't far from reality: they were riding on a Sunday afternoon in the country, and he spotted two mules on the other side of the fence. For the first time in three weeks he spoke to his wife. "Some of your relatives?" he asked.

She was equal to the occasion: "Yes, on my husband's side."

And back into their stewing silence they went.

Dr. James A. Peterson, professor of sociology at the University of Southern California and a foremost authority on marriage and family life, completed an extensive study of couples who had been married between twenty and thirty-five years. His conclusion was that only six couples out of every hundred were satisfied and fulfilled by their marriage relationship. That makes us wonder: Why?

FACE REALITY

The greatest reason for failure in marriage is unrealistic expectations. The average couple enter marriage expecting a wedding to do what only God can do. It takes God to make a marriage meaningful and fulfilling. He created it. Marriage is not the product of a human pervert; it is the product of a divine plan. And God has specifications for the marriage relationship. To attempt to build a marriage without following that plan is to invite failure. That's why the psalmist said, "Except the Lord build the house, they labor in vain that build it" (Ps. 127:1).

According to my understanding of God's plan, to build a successful marriage you must develop a dynamic companionship with your partner. To focus this clearly, let's begin at the beginning. In Genesis 1, you find the repeated statement: "It was good." In verse 31, "God saw everything that He had made, and, behold, it was very good." But in chapter 2, verse 18 we see a startling contrast as He says, "It was *not good* that man should be alone." This is one of the most remarkable statements in the Scriptures. Adam had a perfect environment—no ecological problems there. He had creative genius and all of the responsibility that he could handle. He had unbroken fellowship with the infinite God. But God (not Adam) said, "It's not good that man should be alone."

Man is incomplete without the woman. No other creature could satisfy Adam's aloneness; he had needs only a woman could supply. So God put Adam to sleep, fashioned a woman from a rib, and placed her in front of the man.

I'd like to improve on the *King James* rendering of Adam's reaction: "This is now bone of my bones" (Gen. 2:23). The Hebrew text more accurately says: "Here, now, at last!" Or as we might exclaim: "Where have you been all my life!" Adam immediately recognized Eve as the answer to his aloneness, a partner with a nature like his own to form a helping relationship.

Verse 24 states an action so fundamental in life that both Jesus Christ and the Apostle Paul later repeated it: "Therefore shall a man leave his father and his mother and shall cleave unto his wife." Reflect on the fact that God said this to Adam and Eve *before* they had any children; to two people who never had to break any family ties and therefore had no learning precedent. This is essential parental preparation. The strong human link of children to parents is thus superceded by the unique relationship of husband to wife.

Strangely, in English there are two words, *cleave*, with almost opposite meanings. As a kid in Philadelphia I used a cleaver on a pork chop and made two out of one. The "cleaving" of marriage, however, makes one out of two. The Hebrew word means "to glue, to adhere to"—a separation-proof relationship. God's ideal is one man for one woman for life, and divorce is not a live option.

I wonder when we are going to teach this to our young people. If a young couple comes into marriage thinking that divorce is a live option, the possibilities of their securing one are increased. Scripture declares that marriage is a commitment to each other for life. If we make it less, we pay the consequences.

Another component of the ideal marriage cited in Genesis 2:24 is that the couple shall be—or become—one flesh. The Hebrew text makes clear that this is only begun, not completed, at the time of marriage. This is a process which continues as long as life continues, the cultivating of a one-flesh relationship.

All of my counseling in marriage and family problems can be categorized on the basis of these three situations: failure to truly leave the parents; failure to cleave to the one partner; or failure to develop a unified relationship. The last involves much more than the sexual relationship. A good sexual relationship does not insure a good marriage; rather, a good marriage insures a meaningful sexual relationship. Intimacy, openness, and honesty are qualities that add depth and excitement to the one flesh relationship as years go by.

The secret of my own life and ministry is the one flesh relationship with my wife which God brought into being and is nurturing. It is my greatest satisfaction in life, and it's all of Him. I have no other explanation for it.

WORK AT IT

Is your wife—or husband—your best friend? It's amazing how we sometimes reserve the worst for the one we love the most. I had a businessman in my office who was having problems with his marriage. I said, "What do you do for a living?"

"Oh, I sell insurance—I'm a million-dollar man."

I asked, "How do you sell your insurance?"

"Mostly over coffee or at luncheons. That's the place to sell."

"When is the last time you took out your most important client?"

"What do you mean?"

"Your wife . . . the last time you took her out as a special appointment?"

If I had hit him on the head with a two-by-four, I wouldn't have jarred him more. He said to me later, "It was just like someone pulling a curtain back. Here I spend all my life giving attention to people and I never see my wife in the same perspective!"

Some parents have the opposite problem. I'm very concerned that many young couples are spending their entire lives building their marriages and home around their children. Half of our married years will be spent without children, and the highest incidence of divorce in America is in the forty-five to fifty-five age-group. Why? They're out of kids, and suddenly they look at each other—and discover they're strangers. They have taken no time to cultivate their own relationship, listen to each other, and develop common interests.

How can you cultivate your love life? You have to work at it: a lot of skill, a lot of heart, and a lot of Spirit control are required. To plumb the depths of a love relationship, you must forget yourself and flow into the life of the other person.

If you really want to gauge the quality of your spiritual life, check your love dimensions. Not how often you read the Bible, not how much Scripture you have memorized, but whether the people with whom you are living regard you as a lover—a person refracting the love of Christ which He sheds into your heart.

Before the marriage, the "lover" runs around to the other side of the car to open the door for his beloved. After the marriage, he growls: "What's the matter—you got a broken arm?" Before marriage, he brings flowers. Afterward: "Save them for the funeral." Before marriage, he brings delectable candy. Now: "Aw, she's too fat already." The romance has come to a screeching halt.

I counseled a couple in my office who were having a knock-down, drag-out war of words just before they came in. Every time I would ask the wife a question, the husband would start babbling. And when I asked him a question, she'd lecture. Finally I said, "We have to get some ground rules, OK?" So we tried to do that for half an hour and got nowhere. Then I sent her out, and I said to the man, "Do you love your wife?"

He sat up in his chair as if I had insulted him. "Of course I love my wife," he snapped.

I said, "That's wonderful to know. When's the last time you told her?"

"Do I have to *tell* her?" he groaned.

"No, you don't have to, but it might help. I suggest that when you break the news, though, you first get her into an overstuffed chair so you don't produce a coronary."

He stiffened and shot back, "Mr., Twenty-three years ago I told that woman I loved her, and that's still in effect till I revoke it!"

That case sounded ready for legal proceedings in more ways than one. When was the last time you told your husband or your wife of your love—or are you too sophisticated for that?

Are you man enough to take your wife's face in your hands and say, "I thank God for the privilege of being your husband"?

Or can you as a wife say, "I'm so thankful to God that you're mine"?

What I'm saying in effect is: *Do you have a magnet in your home?* If you don't, there's always the possibility of a magnet developing outside the home. The thing that draws me irresistibly from all over the world back to a little house on Silverrock Drive in Dallas is the lovely woman who is my magnet. Nothing else on earth compares with the pulling power of that magnet for me.

A student came to me some time ago and said, "Prof, I love my wife too much."

"You what?"

"I love my wife too much."

"You gotta be kidding."

"No, I think I do."

So I opened my Bible to the Ephesians 5 passage where it says husbands should love their wives as Christ loved the church. "Do you love her that much?" I asked.

"Oh, no, of course not."

"Well, friend, you had better get with it," I urged.

That, husbands, is our assignment. And it takes the supernatural grace of God. We Americans have a ridiculous idea of what masculinity is. My Bible teaches me that the most masculine person who ever walked the earth was a Man moved with compassion. He shed tears at the loss of a loved one. When He was reviled, He didn't lash back. That takes a man. The mark of Jesus Christ is the mark of tenderness. We need an army of men who are tender not only toward the Saviour but toward their wives, their children, and others.

UNCONDITIONAL LOVE

We're inclined to think that love should vary according to performance, and that people need to change before we can love them more. That isn't God's kind of love, and it isn't the way to change someone. If you're trying to change your partner, stop! Instead, ask God to change *you.*

A lady in our community learned to pray that way and was the instrument to lead her husband to Christ. At Thanksgiving we had a testimony time in our church, and this husband got up and said, "As most of you know, I've been an unbeliever all of my life until this year, when God so worked in the life of my wife that I capitulated to reality."

He sat down and his wife got up and said, "I have to give you the other side of the testimony. When I first went to see Mr. Hendricks, I prayed, 'Lord, *You* love my husband, and *I'll* change him.' And nothing happened. Then I came to the place where I cried out, 'God, *I'll* love him and *You* change him.' And God changed both of us!"

The Book of Ephesians tells us how to live a heavenly life in a hell-like world. Beginning with chapter 4, we have God's orthopedic clinic; this teaches us how to walk through war-stricken territory. "Let all bitterness, and wrath, and anger, and clamor, and evil speaking, be put away from you, with all malice" (Eph. 4:31). Are any of these negative things in your system? Are you willing to give them up?

I know a man who lost a child. He had been digging into the Word of God and sharing his thoughts with others about God's sovereignty. Then this father turned bitter and his spiritual life sagged. He was saying in effect: "God, I'll serve You as long as You do what I want." If God approved him on that basis, he would be headed for hell like the rest of us. But he is learning, as we all must, God's lessons of unconditional love.

Recently he has been emerging from his hurt and pain, sharing with others readily about a God who restores. He never hurts us without healing, never takes away without replacing, renewing, and reaffirming His love for us.

Do you love unconditionally or on a Brownie-point system? Do you try to punish your mate by withdrawing your love? That's not love—at least not love to match the infinite value of your mate.

Notice the positive side of Paul's prescription. "Be ye kind one to another, tenderhearted, forgiving one another, even as God for Christ's sake hath forgiven you" (Eph. 4:32).

When's the last time you said to your partner: "Sweetheart, forgive me; I was acting like a child and I know it"?

SUPERNATURAL CHANGE

There's another aspect that is more important than all the rest. Imagine a triangle, with the top angle representing the Lord and the other angles representing the husband and the wife in their interrelationships. Your vertical relationship with God will always affect your horizontal marital relationship.

I see this pattern followed consistently: first, you are out of fellowship with the Lord; second, you try to compensate by gaining extra concessions from your mate; third, you become self-preoccupied and ask, "What am *I* getting out of this?"

How does a person break out of that ugly, home-wrecking pattern? The most permanent and productive changes in life come through the supernatural. When God works you have proof positive that you have encountered deep reality. Take the case of a football player friend of mine:

God had opened a ministry for me with the Dallas Cowboys football team. The first time I spoke to these men one of them professed faith in Jesus Christ as his Saviour. Then I started a Bible study class for some of the players and their wives. The new Christian called me before going to summer training camp and said, "Hey, Howie, you got something I can work on?"

I said, "Yeah, man, let me give you an assignment. Why don't you dig into the Book of Ephesians? This is a book that's a little rough, but, man, it's where life's at."

He said OK, and I gave him a modern translation for the project.

The day the Cowboy team got back into town my friend was on the phone. "Howie, I've got to see you."

"Fine. Come on over." So he came over.

He said, "Boy, I really got wiped out in the Ephesians stuff. It got serious, especially back here in this last part. I'll find it." He flipped the pages and found the verse: "Husbands, love your wives as Christ loves the church." He looked up. "Man, no way. Frankly, that's impossible."

I said, "Why?"

"Did it ever occur to you that in my profession of football, all my life has been built around me? I've been the center of attraction. It wasn't until I became a Christian that I recognized how utterly self-centered I am. I'll take on any guy or combination of guys in the 'pit'—but in my home I'm the shyest guy in America. And now the Bible tells me to love my wife as Christ loves the church. That's going to take some doing. Have you got any suggestions?"

"Well," I said, "what does your wife do that you really appreciate?"

"Oh," he said, "all kinds of things."

"Well, name one."

"Oh, for example, she's a fantastic cook."

"The next time she makes you a good meal," I directed, "tell her how much you appreciate it." He looked as if I'd asked him to commit murder. I said, "Well, do you think God has enough grace to help you?" He kinda thought God did. "OK," I said, "let's get down on our knees and pray about it."

He poured out his heart: "O God, I'm so self-centered and You know it's going to take a miracle for me to do this. But I guess that's what You specialize in, so I'm trusting You."

That night his wife created one of the best meals she'd ever made—candlelight, the works. But he couldn't enjoy it. When he told me about it later, he said, "I was sitting there in agony, praying for strength to talk. After the meal I got up and went around the table and grabbed my wife—and she went as white as a sheet. I guess she thought I would cripple her. I lifted her up and said, 'Wife, that was wonderful!' "

He called me recently and said, "Howie, this is the real thing."
I said, "How do you know?"

"Man, if Jesus Christ can take a selfish guy like me and teach me how to love my wife, this must be the real thing."

And it is. Or is it—with you? Are you courageous enough, or humble enough, to open yourself to this love of God for your mate?

WITH YOUR CHILDREN

Chapter Nine

Socrates used to say that he wondered how men who were so careful in the training of a colt could be so indifferent to the training of their own children. Certainly the Word of God does not countenance an attitude of indifference toward children.

"Children are an heritage of the Lord," we read in Psalm 127:3. In Proverbs 22:6 we find a staggering promise: "Train up a child in the way he should go: and when he is old, he will not depart from it." That promise has never been canceled nor superseded by any higher truth. Like many of God's promises, it is inseparably linked with a command. It is God's responsibility to fulfill the promise, and it is *our* responsibility to fulfill the command by His enabling grace.

In line with New Testament truth, "training up a child" involves leading him to Christ as Saviour, preferably at an early age. To expect the child to live the Christian life when he does not possess that life is to mock him. The Christian life is not a difficult life—it is an impossible life apart from Christ's leading and power. Not until the Holy Spirit takes up His residence in an individual can that person live so as to please God.

It has been my privilege through the years to lead hundreds of people to Jesus Christ as Saviour, but I have had no greater joy than leading two of my children to Christ and seeing my wife lead the other two into a personal relationship with Him. Conversely, I can think of nothing more tragic than arriving in heaven and discovering that while hundreds came to know Christ because of my ministry, my own four children were lost because of my neglect and preoccupation.

A biblical picture of this child-training process is seen in Paul's words to Timothy as rendered in *The Living Bible*. "But you must keep on believing the things you have been taught. You know they are true, for you know you can trust those of us who have taught you. You know how, when you were a small child, you were taught the Holy Scriptures; and it is these that make you wise to accept God's salvation by trusting in Christ Jesus" (2 Tim. 3:14-15).

Paul also said, "I know how much you trust the Lord, just as your mother Eunice and your grandmother Lois do; and I feel sure you are still trusting Him as much as ever" (2 Tim. 1:5). Here is an illustration of spiritual genetics. A godly grandmother communicated to her daughter, who in turn communicated to Timothy. The mother laid a spiritual fire in the early, impressionable years, and the Spirit of God later ignited that fire as Timothy came into a saving relationship with Christ.

The verb *to train up* occurs only three other times in the Scriptures, and each time it is translated "to dedicate." It was used in context of Solomon's dedicating the temple, and so it means "to set aside for spiritual purposes."

STIMULATE THEIR DESIRE
This training is further explained by the root of the Hebrew verb. It was used to describe the process of the Hebrew midwife who, at the time of birth, would plunge a finger into crushed dates and olive oil and rub the substance across the roof of the mouth of the newborn infant. The child was stimulated to suck and take nourishment, and this came to be translated: "create a desire."

How hungry and thirsty are you making your children for Jesus Christ? Somebody says, "You ought to know you can lead a horse to water, but you can't make him drink." That's right, but you can feed him salt! That's what I am suggesting. Your life ought to demonstrate the reality and the day-to-day relevance of Christian faith so that your children want it. Only as you possess that reality do you have something significant to say. The present generation is weary of words; they are screaming for reality.

We had a lovely couple in Dallas a number of years ago. He sold his business at a loss, went into vocational Christian work, and things got rather rough. There were four kids in the family. One night at family worship, Timmy, the youngest boy, said, "Daddy, do you think Jesus would mind if I asked Him for a shirt?"

"Well, no, of course not. Let's write that down in our prayer request book, Mother."

So she wrote down "shirt for Timmy" and she added "size seven." You can be sure that every day Timmy saw to it that they prayed for the shirt. After several weeks, one Saturday the mother received a telephone call from a clothier in downtown Dallas, a Christian businessman. "I've just finished my July clearance sale, and knowing that you have four boys, it occurred to me that you might use something we have left. Could you use some boy's shirts?"

She said, "What size?"

"Size seven."

"How many do you have?" she asked hesitantly.

He said, "Twelve."

Many of us might have taken the shirts, stuffed them in the bureau drawer, and made some casual comment to the child. Not this wise set of parents. That night, as expected, Timmy said, "Don't forget, Mommy, let's pray for the shirt."

Mommy said, "We don't have to pray for the shirt, Timmy."

"How come?"

"The Lord has answered your prayer."

"He has?"

"Right." So, as previously arranged, brother Tommy goes out and gets one shirt, brings it in, and puts it down on the table. Little Timmy's eyes are like saucers. Tommy goes out and gets another shirt and brings it in. Out—back, out—back, until he piles twelve shirts on the table, and Timmy thinks God is going into the shirt business. But you know, there is a little kid in Dallas today by the name of Timothy who believes there is a God in heaven interested enough in his needs to provide boys with shirts.

Do your kids know that? That's fantastic communication. That, by the way, is one of the dangers of living in an affluent society. Don't gripe because your income isn't what you would like it to be. Thank God, it may be the greatest blessing that ever happened to your family, especially to your children. I have spent too much time around very wealthy individuals who would give their right arms if they could get their children back.

So child training begins with the parents. And we do well to look at God's first and preeminent commandment: "Thou shalt love the Lord thy God with all thine heart, and with all thy soul, and with all thy might" (Deut. 6:5).

Are you in love with the living Lord? Do you love Him more than you did yesterday? Is He more prominent in your life than in the days after you were born of the Spirit of God into His family?

Every day I get up I have to fall in love afresh with Jesus Christ. I have to cultivate this relationship just as I have to cultivate my relationship with my wife. This does not come by accident. And unless I have this love in my heart, I will not have it in my home. That is what Moses told Israel.

"These words, which I command you, shall be in *thine heart;* and thou shalt teach them diligently unto thy children" (Deut. 6:6-7). First in *my* heart, then in my children's. And Moses said to teach *diligently*—that means to throw everything you have into the task.

After visiting a home where the family's love for each other was deeply refreshing, a friend and I walked toward my car, and he said, "Some people have the most wonderful children—some people do, some people don't." Just then I noticed a neatly manicured lawn, and I responded, "Some people have the most beautiful lawns even in August."

He looked at me and said slowly: "If you have a beautiful lawn in August in Texas, you have worked at it."

Yes, good lawns and good families take *work*.

UNDERSTAND THEIR NEEDS AND FEELINGS

Homes are coming apart because their members are; that is, everyone moves within his separate orbit and home becomes the filling station where we check the gas and chassis for replenishment and repair, but we don't spend much time there. Like ships passing in the night, very little life flows from one member to another.

As a marriage and family counselor, I encounter some very interesting cases. Some time ago a boy was picked up by a police squad car, and the first thing he said to the officer was, "You aren't going to tell my old man, are you?"

He replied, "I'd be interested in hearing why you don't want your father to know."

"I'll tell you," he answered. "He's not interested in me; he's too busy."

When the policeman called the father about his son, the irate response was: "What in the world are you calling me for?"

The case was referred to me, and it was my privilege to lead the father to Jesus Christ. He became a different person, and he became concerned about his family problems.

He came to my office one day and said, "OK, now what do I do? Let's put this thing back together."

"Friend, this is going to take time," I warned him. "You can't decimate the bridges for fifteen years and rebuild them overnight. What does your son like to do?"

He had to think for a long time but finally came up with, "He likes to go fishing."

I said, "OK, why don't you plan a fishing trip with him?"

He went home and in typical adult fashion announced: "Son, next week we are going fishing."

The boy looked him in the eye and said, *"You're* going fishing. I've already got some things planned."

The father blew his top. He gave the boy a portion of his mind he couldn't really afford to lose, and the son countered very calmly: "A number of years ago I wanted to go fishing, and you were too busy. Now you want to go fishing, and I'm too busy. What's your problem?"

The father came back to my office like a whipped dog to find out what he could do. He was so low he began to realize he must trust God to do what he himself could not. He could appreciate the fact that his family needed to *understand* each other, not just talk at each other.

Sometimes I encounter a family where communications are so frozen that I get them all in my office and we start a conversation. I only allow one person to talk at a time, and after one expresses himself, I ask another member: "Now tell me what you heard him say." And we stick to that until everyone in the group can say back to the satisfaction of the speaker what he said. It's painful and time-consuming, but it's amazing how for the first time they begin to hear what the individual is really saying. Then they have the possibility of communicating.

Some parents thoroughly involve their children in the father's work. I was in the home of a Chicago executive and had wonderful fellowship with the whole family. In the kitchen I saw the walls plastered with the advertising of the executive's company, and I said, "Well, you do have a promotional program here."

"No," he replied, "that's my ministry. We pray for that as a family."

That's vastly different from the family that speaks of the factory or the office or what-have-you as the "monster" that is supposedly ruining their lives.

ENJOY LIFE WITH THEM

In Deuteronomy 6:7 there are two key terms which spell out the nature of parental education. One is *teach* (that's formal, structured). The other is *talk* (that's informal, situational). A good parent uses both kinds of instruction, realizing that informal times together are actually teaching situations, for good or ill.

Do you take the time and make the effort to have fun in your home? Do your kids enjoy their home? To me, the poorest representative of Jesus Christ is the Christian who doesn't know what it is to enjoy life. Many of us are so glum we look as if we're on the road to hell instead of the road to heaven. The only people in the world today who are in a position to laugh and rejoice are those who are secure in Jesus Christ!

I can remember in the early days of my family recreation we started out with a tent. My wife was not exactly the tenting type, but it's amazing what you can get used to. Now that my children are pretty well grown, it is interesting to ask what they remember most. The two boys remember when they and I stayed in a pup tent—talk about togetherness; it was wall-to-wall!

Before we went to bed that night, I looked to the west and said, "Hey, fellows, you'd better dig those trenches deep around the edge; it looks like we may get some rain." Well, we got nine inches of rain in four hours. And we ended up two miles down the creek, drying ourselves out under a shelter and talking about the Lord and His protective hand. Back in Dallas, we found out later, thirteen people died that night from the storm. You know, that lesson in God's protection wasn't sermon number 293 in my file; that was real life, and it communicated!

One of the great fun times in our home has been the Friday night "Hendricks Talent Theater." We would put old clothes and junk in a bag and drag them out for an unrehearsed drama. Television was boring beside our production. I came out of those experiences with my ribs sore from laughing. Have you ever examined the atmosphere of your home and asked how attractive it is? You say, "I'm so glad you asked; we just finished decorating it. Man, we've got wall-to-wall carpeting, coordinating drapes."

No, I didn't ask you that—that's your junk. I asked you, how attractive is your home? I go into many Christian homes today and, frankly, I am repelled. They are covered over with legalism. There is what I call a suffocating fog of moralism, and every time the kid moves we're nailing him to the floor. Every time he turns around we're cramming something down his throat. "All right, let's get together; we're going to have Bible study now." Not too long ago, one dear lady blew her cork in the midst of the family worship. She shouted at the kids, "Shut up; you ought to hear what God has to say!" Some of us say "shut up" so many times, our children are like the kid who was eight years old before he discovered his name was not Shut Up. What are you like to live with?

We had two students at the seminary from a home in California that has sent all its children into Christian work. Some time ago I was with one of them and I asked: "What do you remember most about your father?"

He thought for a minute and then said, "Two things stand out in my mind, and they're quite contrasting. The first thing is getting up early in the morning for a paper route and seeing my father on his knees praying. That made a profound impression on me. The second thing is him rolling on the floor with laughter with us kids!" What a combination—on the floor in prayer and on the floor in laughter! By the way—what will your children remember you for?

LIVE HONESTLY BEFORE THEM

The atmosphere of the home inculcates Christian truth more effectively than the words we speak. The attitude of truthfulness, for example, is more caught than taught. A student asked me sometime ago what I thought was the most important trait for my children to gain. I told him I'd have to think about that a while, and I came to the conclusion that if I had to choose only one characteristic for my children, it would be honesty. I want children who are honest to God, to other people, and honest with themselves. And I realized it is most likely to be conveyed through example.

The phone rings. It's for Tom. Tom's wife, Mary, asks with her hand securely covering the mouthpiece, "Tom, are you here?"

Tom deceitfully replies, "No, I'm not here!"

Now, you can tell your child all you want about honesty, but you are teaching him to be a first-class liar.

I find that young people from Christian homes are rebelling most over phoniness and lack of reality, not from having parents who are not perfect. I find that the parent who is honest enough to admit "Buddy, I goofed; I apologize" comes over like horseradish.

Let's suppose that I were to tell you I sell the best hair restorer lotion in existence—it's guaranteed. You take another look at my bald head and go into hysterics. Should I blame you? But this is what is happening in many Christian homes. Parents are trying to teach truth and love for God when they don't possess them. If the reality of Jesus Christ has not gripped you, you cannot pass it on to your children. I sometimes think we might communicate Christ better to our children if we were deaf and dumb because we would realize how much we need Jesus Christ helping us.

I have trouble with this too. I can understand that I need the control of the Holy Spirit to address a crowd, or to witness, or to teach a Bible class. But who needs the control of the Spirit for playing a game with the kids? Paul says, "Whatsoever you do in word or in deed, do all in the name of the Lord Jesus" (Col. 3:17). There's only one way we can do that, and that's under the Spirit's control.

When I had the privilege of speaking to 8,000 people at a Sunday School convention in California, my students told me they'd be praying for me. I felt it, and the good results were obviously from God. Then I caught a plane back to Dallas. After my wife welcomed me back, she got down to reality and said, "Honey, I've got bad news for you. The sewer has broken."

"Did you call the repairman?"

"Four times. He says it's caved in."

"Well, let's get it fixed."

"He said it will cost $425 to dig a trench out to the alley."

"Not $425! I'll dig it myself."

So I enlisted my son—he's a physical fitness buff—and we went to work. If you've ever dug in Texas gumbo, you know it's like concrete. We got out six or eight feet and discovered the pipe was going in a downward direction! We dug in again, and finally we came to the break—sure enough, it was caved in. We stood there in the trench meditating and suddenly someone flushed the toilet!

Was the Holy Spirit with me in that soggy trench—as He had been when I was speaking to 8,000 people about Christian truth? If not, I don't have much to talk about. If the Holy Spirit doesn't control your temper at the office or your tongue when you're around godless people, then we shouldn't talk about having the fullness of the Spirit. He has to work in the nitty-gritty of life, or He isn't working in us.

Some of my toughest tests come at home—after God has used me in a public ministry to other people. And the more you try to live distinctly for Jesus Christ, the more you will understand what reality is—because you'll face the basic issues and find you can't handle them except in Jesus' power.

"Whom the Lord loves, He chasteneth" (Heb. 12:6). Is God disciplining you? He loves you, and He has saved you so you may be conformed to the image of His Son. We remember that even Jesus learned obedience by the things that He suffered. Your children have a great need for adequate models—are you one? Neither am I—that's why the Lord is working on us.

EXPRESS LOVE FOR THEM

Another thing we parents can work on is expressing our love for one another. I hope you're not ashamed to express your love in front of your children. The best thing a father can do for his son is to love his son's mother; the best thing a mother can do for her daughter is to love her daughter's father. In this context the children learn to give and receive love for each other. And you'll never develop a pervert in this kind of environment.

Do you get shook up over your kids fighting? My counsel as a veteran referee is: don't sweat it. Our children had some knock-down, drag-out skirmishes—our own Civil War. They are now grown and married, and I dare anyone to scowl at my daughter when her brother is around. They are so close that tears roll down their faces when they greet one another at an airport, and they couldn't care less what others think of their affection.

How do you develop love? It comes over a period of time and as a product of a pattern. We can do a lot of things to encourage the expression of love.

Birthdays have always been significant in our home. I remember when my girls were learning to cook, and the younger one decided she would make doughnuts for Bob's birthday. They turned out like rocks; every time you'd swallow a bite you could hear the splash. But Bob ate the last one of those doughnuts, hugged his sister, and said, "Man, what a cook you are, Bev."

Once I had a poignant experience in an unexpected place. I was in an opulent home—probably in the million dollar class. It belongs to a man who told me: "I ended up at the top of my field but at the bottom of life." Then he found Jesus Christ as his Saviour, and he and his wife began studying the Word to find out how the Lord wanted them to train their children.

I went into their gorgeous living room and almost got lost in the living room rug—felt like I might get a severe case of mink rash on the spot. Interior designers have convinced us that a living room has to have a center of interest, but right in the center of that lovely room was a peanut butter jar holding wilted daisies. I found out that her son had picked them for her on his way home from school, and I said, "I bet they have a lot of meaning to you."

She beamed and said, "That's the most wonderful thing in this room."

My wife taught me that a relationship is far more important than a clean home. We can have a *Better Homes and Gardens* layout and a *Mad* family life. The floor can be quickly cleaned after little feet have muddied it, but bruised relationships are not so easily restored.

Occasionally I have had the assignment of going into an exclusive home in Dallas and telling the parents that the court has decided to put away their child permanently. When these people have no internal resources, they come unglued at the seams. We had one boy in custody who drove the most expensive brand sports car in America and had a monthly allowance of $475. He had just about everything except parents who gave of themselves. The stuff you buy will never substitute for you; there is no substitute for a personal, loving relationship in the family.

You know what I have to do? People call me on the phone. "Prof, will you come over and preach to us?"

"No, I'm awfully sorry, I won't."

"You won't? How come?"

Well, I've learned to say, "I'm otherwise engaged," which, being interpreted, means, "I'm going to stay home."

A few years ago I used to be a little more direct. Somebody would call up and say, "Would you come over and preach for us?"

"No, I'm awfully sorry. I can't come that night."

"How come?"

"I'm going to stay home and play with my kids."

"You what?"

"I'm going to stay home and play with my kids."

"You mean you're not coming to preach to us?"

"No, I'm not coming to preach to you."

Somebody says, "Oh, that's how liberalism gets started in the seminary." And if I listen to that kind of garbage I could lose my whole family in the process. We must not allow anybody to control our lives except the Spirit of God, and there is no conflict between duty and Christian experience. Your call to be a parent is not in conflict with your call to be a Christian. If it is, you should have remained a celibate!

I don't know what my kids will remember me for. I hope they will be able to remember me as a father who loved them and enjoyed them. I believe the greatest challenge confronting Christian fathers today is to become articulate concerning our faith so we can communicate it to our children. Our homes should be laboratories for instructing our children formally and informally. Homes should be training grounds for developing habit patterns that serve Jesus Christ. And then we'll avoid the tragedy described in Judges 2:10— a generation arose which knew not the Lord.

IN YOUR CHURCH

Chapter Ten

The contemporary Christian church is suffering from a severe case of identity crisis. It's like an amnesia victim trying to find out: "Who am I?" And it is aggravated by the fact that the organized church is under fire from both outsiders and insiders. In fact, someone has said that the church is like Noah's ark: "If it weren't for the storm on the outside, you couldn't stand the stench on the inside."

Frequently I am asked, "Is there any future for the church?" That depends. Whose church are you talking about? Your church? I can't guarantee your church for the next month, but if you mean Christ's church, it will never fail. Jesus Christ said, "I will build My church, and the gates of hell shall not prevail against it" (Matt. 16:18). He expected there would be opposition and difficulty and problems, but His church would prevail. It's a winner.

But the question nags, "Why is the organized church failing? I believe that the church fails when it attempts to do what other human institutions can do instead of what only the church can do and what God has called it to do.

There are several misconceptions about the church that we need to erase from our thinking. To many people, the church is a building. You ask an individual: "Where is your church?"

"Fourth and Main."

That's not Christ's church. That's just the place where a cell of the church gathers. To some people, the local church is a program something like that offered by a country club. You pay for the privilege of participation, but you can take it or leave it. If you want to swim or play tennis or eat, you may, but you're under no obligation so long as you pay your dues. I'm afraid the program has become paramount in many churches today and has depersonalized people instead of enriching them.

To other people church is like a stadium or theater where they go to watch the professionals perform for a price. The spectators watch the actors do their thing. Of course, the local church produces a little involvement at the door when the people shake the pastor's hand and say, "It was a wonderful sermon," and he's assured he has earned his keep for another week.

In contrast, the Word of God teaches us that Christ's church is people—born-again people. They may meet in a building, they may have a program, they may render services to others, and gifted men among them may equip believers for their individual ministries. But the church of Jesus Christ is none of those things; it is the people. His church exists wherever believers are.

The Apostle Paul's favorite analogy of the church in both Corinthians and Ephesians is the body. It pulsates with life: Jesus Christ is its Head, and you and I as believers are its members. The members are gifted in order to function as an organism and organization, and they have the opportunity for rich fellowship with each other. The characteristics of this body determine what the church does, so we should know the characteristics of the church as it is found in the New Testament.

A PRAYING BODY

First, the church is a praying body. This is seen in Acts 4:31: "And when they had prayed, the place was shaken where they were assembled together; and they were all filled with the Holy Ghost, and they spake the Word of God with boldness." In the middle of a prayer meeting, the church members were filled with the Spirit and liberated so they could speak the Word of God fearlessly. This Book of Acts, you know, is the only "unfinished" book in the Bible. You and I are adding new "chapters" every day to this history of the Christian church. And we must never abandon prayer, the church's means of power.

In the course of a year, I minister to many kinds of churches. An interesting fact is that all these different church groups claim they are "New Testament churches." And yet the identifying marks of New Testament Christianity are sometimes scarce, if not absent, in them.

Notice the life of the church in Acts 2:41-42: "Then they that gladly received his word were baptized; and the same day there were added unto them about 3,000 souls. And they continued steadfastly in the apostles' doctrine and fellowship, and in breaking of bread and in [the] prayers." There should be that definite article *the* with "prayers." Apparently there were times when they met together specifically for prayer.

A New Testament kind of church is a school, a training center where people are equipped for their personal ministry to others. It's a gathering place for fellowship, and that does not mean "coffee and doughnuts." Did you ever wonder how the early church managed to have fellowship without coffee and doughnuts? It must have been difficult! But today we can join so-called fellowship groups and not find an ounce of the real thing. There we talk about the weather, sports scores, the new taxes—about almost everything in the world except the Lord Jesus Christ and our life with Him.

When did you last experience New Testament fellowship? Perhaps in "the breaking of bread" where we remember the death of our Lord Jesus Christ? How about "in [the] prayers"? Prayer is not an option to the church; it's an essential. Prayer is not a luxury; it's our survival gear. It's our spiritual breathing apparatus—and some of us are gasping for air. I have been in churches where elders have been afraid to pray after thirty years as church officers. How can this be so?

We have false ideas about prayer. We think that prayer involves certain lingo. And the "professionals" who have been to Bible school or seminary can pray better than other Christians, of course. You couldn't guess how many times I've visited a meeting of Christians and been called on to pray—and I've had the strongest urge to get up and say: "Isn't there anybody else around here who can pray?"

There are two kinds of people I love to hear pray. One is children, and the other is new converts. Their prayers are so refreshing and so honest. I had a scholar in my home for the evening meal and our family worship afterward. My kids were very small at the time and they prayed for the typical things. They thanked Jesus for the yard fence, for the sand pile, and the dog. I could sense this was disturbing to our guest, and he could hardly wait to question me later.

He said, "Professor Hendricks, you don't mean to tell me that a teacher at a theological seminary teaches his children to pray for things like that?"

"Oh," I said, "I certainly do. Do you ever pray about your income?"

"Oh, certainly," he said.

"Well, do you think your income is more important to God than my boy's tricycle? Do you ever pray for protection?"

"Oh, I never get into my car that I don't pray about the hazards of the highway."

"That is what my boy is praying about when he prays for the fence that keeps big dogs on the other side."

I didn't tell the scholar this, but I think many of us are educated beyond our intelligence!

We led a fellow to faith in Christ at a home Bible study class, then we told him he should build on this foundation by attending a church where he would have good instruction and fellowship. He took us at our word and showed up for church on Sunday morning and evening. Then he came to Wednesday night Bible study—and there he ran into a problem.

After taking notes and drinking in the message like a sponge, this fellow stopped me when we were dividing up into prayer groups and said, "Howie, I've got a problem. I can't pray the way you guys say it."

"That's no problem," I reassured him. "Thank God you don't pray like us!"

He didn't quite understand that, and I knew he felt hesitant to participate. After some time I put my hand on his knee and squeezed, and I'll never forget the prayer that came out. He said something like: "Lord, this is Jim. I'm the one that met You last Thursday night over at _____ (I really thought he was going to give God his zip code too!). I hope You'll forgive me 'cause I can't say it the way these guys can. Maybe if I know You as long as they do, I'll do a better job, but I'd like You to know from the bottom of my heart, I really do love You. Thanks, Lord. Amen."

That new believer turned on a prayer meeting after the others had "said prayers."

There's a surprising amount of humor in the Bible, and Acts 12 is a case in point. It starts out in tragedy: King Herod is on a rampage, and he kills James, then locks Peter in prison with the intention of making him a second martyr. But earnest prayer was going up for Peter—and God's angel set him free! That really caused problems, as we see in verse 12:

"He [Peter] came to the house of Mary the mother of John, whose surname was Mark, where many were gathered together praying. And as Peter knocked at the door of the gate, a damsel came to hearken, named Rhoda, and when she knew Peter's voice, she opened not the gate for gladness, but ran in, and told how Peter stood before the gate."

Get the picture? Here they are praying, "O Lord, You gotta

deliver Peter." So here he is waiting to get in, and they tell the excited girl, "Hush! You're mad!" But she couldn't keep quiet, and they found another explanation: "It's Peter's angel." I guess that seemed more believable, because nobody was praying for his angel to appear!

But "Peter continued knocking." If I know Peter, he was pounding that door by now. The last part of verse 16 almost wipes me out: "When they had opened the door and saw him they were astonished." That's a tame translation! This is the strongest Greek word for utter amazement—they were figuratively knocked out!

Well, how about yourself? If a friend came up to you and said, "The answer you've been praying about for ten years has come!" would you believe it? Too often we don't expect God to do much about our prayers—and we're seldom disappointed! That's because one of the keys to successful prayer is that you believe. God specializes in the impossible—something that's hard for us experienced adults to understand! That's why I love working with kids. They pray for the most staggering things while I try to help them be reasonable. The first thing you know, the "impossible" is staring us in the face!

A SHARING BODY

A second distinguishing mark of a New Testament church is that it is a sharing body. In Hebrews we see the sharing of a common life, and it's the life of Jesus Christ. In Hebrews 10:24-25 we read: "Let us consider one another to provoke unto love and to good works, not forsaking the assembling of ourselves together as the manner of some is, but exhorting one another, and so much the more as ye see the day approaching."

The Lord has made us very dependent people—not only dependent upon Him but upon each other. When that grips your heart, you will never be the same person in your assembly of believers. You see, there is no room in the true church for the independent; we are all interdependent. And one part of the body cannot say to the other part of the body, "I have no need of you" (1 Cor. 12:21).

I heard of a remarkable dream a man had—rather wild, but with a fantastic message. People were sitting along both sides of a sumptuous banquet table covered with delicious foods of every variety. But everyone had a baffling problem. Their arms were bound to boards and they could not bend their elbows. They managed to reach the food but could not get it in their mouths! Can you imagine anything more frustrating?

Finally one guest swung his arm to the fellow across the table and put his food in the other man's mouth. The second fellow returned the favor, and in no time everyone at the banquet was enjoying a delicious meal. That's your privilege as a Christian—to feed others and to receive from others. Galatians 6:2 says, "Bear ye one another's burdens, and so fulfill the law of Christ." The local church should be a community of concerned people.

I'm an extremely healthy individual, but some years ago I had some major physical problems during a difficult six-month period. I had to cancel an exciting summer conference and "climb the walls" of my bedroom. I couldn't get in any position without agonizing pain. When I finally got back to the classroom, a group of seminary wives said, "How's your health?"

I said, "It's not really too good, to be honest with you."

They said, "Oh, for the last three weeks we have covenanted together to pray for you and your physical needs every day."

The next time I went back to my orthopedic friend, he said, "Hendricks, my only explanation for your recovery is spiritual, not medical."

A corps of women dared to undertake for my physical well-being as a part of their spiritual concern—and I got well! I think one of the most exciting things taking place in churches today is this concern and shared life coming into reality. A great many people are searching for help. They are going down in the surf of adversity, and they don't need somebody on shore shouting: "If you'd listened in the first place you'd never have gotten into that!" They need somebody who is willing to wade into the breakers with prayer and practical assistance before they go down the third time.

A RESTORING COMMUNITY

This leads me to the third distinguishing mark of a New Testament church. It's given in Galatians 6:1: "Brethren, if a man be overtaken in a fault, ye who are spiritual, club him . . ." Is that what it says? That's the *Reversed* Standard Version. It says: ". . . restore such an one. . . ."

Restore is a medical term. It is used in relation to a compound fracture in which the bone is completely displaced and the pieces have to be brought together very delicately and skillfully so they will mend. Paul goes on to say: "Considering thyself, lest thou also be tempted." The church is not the community of the perfect; it's the community of the progressing.

Now and then someone comes to me and says, "Hendricks, can you recommend a church for me?"

"What kind of church are you looking for?" I ask, and he gives me the specifications.

"O friend," I suggest, "you're looking for a perfect church—if you ever find one, don't join because you'll ruin it."

People tell me, "My church has problems." Wonderful—you're undoubtedly making progress. If you have no problems, you're probably paralyzed. The early church had problems. They were loaded with them!

I met a man in Indianapolis who has a remarkable ministry. He has not only led a lot of people to Christ, but he has been very successful in discipling converts. I was having lunch with him, and I said, "Tell me what the Spirit of God has taught you."

He shared a number of things with me, but I'll never forget this. He said, "One of the first things I do with a new convert is to ask if we can get together for lunch soon. We meet and I say, 'How's it going?'

" 'Good. It's really wonderful to know the Lord.'

" 'Having any problems?'

" 'No, man; great.'

" 'Then, would you mind if I shared one of my problems with you?' I ask.

" 'You share *your* problem? *You* led me to Christ.'

"But I start talking about a personal problem, and he identifies with it as his own. I'm convinced that the way to get a new Christian off the launching pad in the spiritual realm is to show him that he is not a person without problems but a person who has the Problem-solver living within."

In many churches we give the impression that when you come to Jesus Christ you automatically get rid of your problems. The result is that when a Christian has a problem he is scared to admit it to anybody, including himself. Galatians 6:1 teaches us that we are committed to a ministry of restoration—speaking to a brother, picking him up along the way, encouraging him, strengthening him, restoring him, so he can go on.

SPIRITUAL GIFTS

The fourth mark of a vital New Testament church is its spiritual gifts. The doctrine of spiritual gifts is probably the most neglected truth among believers today. Romans 12, 1 Corinthians 12, and Ephesians 4 teach us about these gifts. We should saturate our minds with these passages.

Notice Ephesians 4:7—"But unto *every one* of us is given *grace* according to the measure of the *gift* of Christ." These gifts are appropriately called "grace gifts"; the gift is worthless apart from the grace of God with which it functions.

Paul writes further (v. 8), quoting from Psalm 68:18—"When He ascended up on high, He led captivity captive, and gave gifts unto men." God gave each Christian a spiritual gift with which to function in the body. Do you know what your spiritual gift is?

I ask a man, "My friend, what's your spiritual gift?"

He says, "My spiritual gift? I'm a plumber."

"No, I didn't ask your occupation; I'm asking what is your spiritual gift." It's our job to discover, to develop, and to employ our spiritual gift in the body of Christ. And there is no second-class citizen in His body. There is no insignificant gift.

We have Christians running all over with inferiority complexes; they can't do this and they can't do that. But God has given them a gift though they don't know what it is. How insidious Satan is; he cloaks the fact that God has given Christians gifts with which to function in the body.

Some time ago I asked one of the men in the church where I fellowship to lead a home Bible class as I was launching a new one in another area. "Wow," he objected, "I don't have the gift of teaching."

"How do you know, Bill?" I said. "Did God let down a sheet from heaven one night and tell you that?"

"No, no; I just don't have it," he insisted.

"Have you ever taught?" I asked.

"No, I've never taught."

"Then don't tell me you don't have the gift of teaching, my friend, because you don't know that." Today if I want to send my students to see a man who knows how to communicate a lot better than most professionals, I send them out to hear Bill!

Ephesians 4:11-12 tell us how these gifts function. "He gave some, apostles; and some, prophets; and some, evangelists; and some, pastors and teachers; for the perfecting of the saints, for the work of the ministry, for the edifying of the body of Christ."

In spite of this provision, the typical church hires a clergyman to rob them of the privilege of exercising Christ's gifts. The reason God gave the gift of pastor-teacher is for equipping laymen to do the work God has given them to do. Through this gift we can produce a multiplication of ministries.

Often I get on a plane and get involved in conversation. Everything is going well until someone says, "By the way, what do you do?"

"Well, I'm in education."

"Oh, that's interesting. Where do you teach?"

"I teach at the Dallas Theological Seminary."

"What? Oh, yeah, a preacher!"

He figures I'm a professional Christian, and immediately I'm at a disadvantage. It's like fighting with one arm tied behind my back. I'm paid to be good, they figure, so I could be something else for higher pay. But a Christian housewife, a salesman, a student, a lawyer, or some other layman lives his faith only because he wants to.

Make no mistake: the greatest curse on the church today is that we are expecting a small corps of professionals to get God's work done. No way!

Bud Wilkinson, former football coach at the University of Oklahoma, was in Dallas for a series of lectures on physical fitness. A TV reporter interviewed him about the President's physical fitness program and asked: "Mr. Wilkinson, what would you say is the contribution of modern football to physical fitness?" The reporter expected a lengthy speech.

As if he had been waiting thirty years for this question, he said, "Absolutely nothing."

The young reporter stared and squirmed and finally stuttered, "Would you care to elaborate on that?"

Wilkinson said, "Certainly. I define football as twenty-two men on the field who desperately need rest and 50,000 people in the grandstand who desperately need exercise."

I thought to myself: What a definition of a church! A few compulsively active people run around the field while the mass of the people rest in the stands. But this is not according to the Word of God! God gave us all gifts for using in the body of Christ, not for smothering inactivity. Do you know what your gift is? Are you involved so that you might find out what it is? Are you exercising it, and trying to develop it? You may have a variety of gifts. Discover them and put them into practice.

A WITNESSING BODY

Last, a New Testament kind of church, according to the Word of God, is a witnessing body. In Acts 1:8 we find the last words of Jesus Christ to His disciples while on earth, and they are very significant.

"But ye shall receive power, after that the Holy Ghost is come upon you: and ye shall be witnesses unto Me both in Jerusalem, and in all Judea, and in Samaria, and unto the uttermost part of the earth." Did it ever occur to you as you read through the New Testament that there is a remarkable absence of exhortation to share your faith? I don't think it occurred to the early church *not* to share their faith. And by the end of the Book of Acts the Christians were further toward reaching their world for Christ than we are after these many hundreds of years with all our technological advantages. Why? Because the rank and file Christians were going everywhere witnessing.

Many churches count on the trained professionals to communicate the message of the Gospel. But if you were hailed into court tomorrow and charged with being a Christian, is there enough evidence to convict you?

Wherever I go, I find people of my generation and older who are shook up over what's happening in our country. They say, "You are a student of the Scriptures; do you think it is possible for our country to undergo great persecution?" I tell them I think it is not only possible but very probable for our generation. And I think that might be the greatest boost some of us ever get in stimulating our Christian life.

When I was privileged to minister in India, I spoke at a pastors' conference just outside the state of Assam. Three pastors came who had just been released from prison for preaching the Gospel in Assam. I asked them what it was like there. They said, "Just like the Book of the Acts. The more we were persecuted, the more we prospered. We started two services, then three, four, five services every Sunday morning to accommodate the crowds. Then the elders had to make a rule: persons could come to only one service a Sunday so that other people could attend. Later they had to limit people to attending only every other Sunday! I came away from that encounter wondering how we could launch a persecution!"

It was entirely different at a Campus Crusade staff conference I attended—but just as thrilling. There I met a young lady at dinner and got into a conversation. I said, "Tell me how you became saved."

Her face lit up and she said, "I was a student at the University of Illinois. I didn't have a clue how to get to heaven. Some girls came to our living quarters and shared Jesus Christ with us, and I was wonderfully born again. I went home and the first thing I was privileged to do was to lead my two sisters to Christ."

Their lives were so changed that their mother came to them and said, "You know, I have always thought I was a Christian, but the more I see you in action the more I'm convinced that I don't know what it is all about." So they led their mom to Christ.

Pop was the hold-out: "It's nice for them, but it's not my bag. And, besides, wait until the pressure gets on them."

She went on to tell about her graduation and her marriage to a young man who went to Vietnam as a helicopter pilot. Before long he was shot down in action—killed—and she got the telegram alone. She had no Christian background, and she had never seen anyone go through this kind of experience. She knew one verse of Scripture besides the ones about salvation in the Four Spiritual Laws booklet, and it was, "As thy days, so shall thy strength be" (Deut. 33:25).

She prayed, "Lord, You must have a purpose. I don't really understand, and I'm not even asking You to explain. All I'm asking You for is the strength to get through today." And she was flooded with peace from God. It was totally unexplainable.

The next day she claimed the same promise, and the next day and the next until finally her father called her, "I'm catching a plane.

I've got to see you!" When he arrived he said, "You've got to tell me how to accept Jesus Christ. If He can bring that kind of reality in human experience, I've got to have it."

That's the genius of a witnessing community. Let me ask you as I ask myself: How much reality do you have in your life? You cannot impart what you do not possess. If you are really born again by the Spirit of God, don't make the tragic mistake of being a secret-service Christian.

And if you are a member of Christ's body, a community of concerned people, God has given you a gift. He wants to restore you through that body, strengthen and encourage you, and He wants to use that body as a launching pad to thrust you into your community where people are blind to the glories of Christ and must see Him incarnate in your life.

IN YOUR NEIGHBORHOOD

Chapter Eleven

The Gospel is failing to produce results in some places today because it lacks an audience. Christians in churches are busy evangelizing the evangelized. We constantly face the danger of developing a fortress mentality, making occasional excursions into unfriendly territory and scurrying back to the safety of our church and its people when opposition arises. We tend to derive security from friendly surroundings rather than from Jesus Christ, and so we fail to penetrate our society for Christ.

A friend of mine told me recently, "Howie, we just moved, and the most exciting thing happened—we moved next door to a Christian couple."

I guess I startled her when I said, "How unfortunate!" She didn't understand that, and after some kidding I asked if she'd ever thought God might want her family to evangelize their new neighborhood instead of spending most of their time with another Christian family. She had never thought of that, as most Christians don't. And so we easily become isolated and insulated from the people God intends us to reach.

In Mark 2 we read about Jesus going to the seaside and being

117

surrounded by a multitude, to whom He ministered. But He was not interested only in the multitude; he was concerned about individuals. Jesus spotted a man named Levi at a tax collector's station, and He said to Levi, "Follow Me." Here Jesus Christ identified Himself with a social leper, a man who served the hated Romans at the expense of his countrymen. And then Jesus sat down to a meal with Levi and his notorious cronies.

This is one of the most beautiful pictures in the New Testament to me. Jesus Christ, who knew no sin, who did no sin, and in whom was no sin, put Himself in the midst of sinners in order to communicate to them. When watching Pharisees criticized Him, Jesus said He was meeting with people who needed Him.

TALK THEIR LANGUAGE

There are many ways Christians today can involve themselves in the lives of non-Christians. Perhaps one of the most successful methods is the home Bible study. But it's no good to get sinners into a home Bible study and then try to communicate the Gospel to them in a foreign language.

In Cleveland a few years ago I conducted a workshop on home Bible classes. Only six people came, but one couple went home and prayed: "Lord, forgive us for our isolation from non-Christians. Help us to start penetrating our community for Christ." Though she didn't know how to do the job, the wife started a class in the home of a neighbor who belonged to a formal church but knew nothing of the Bible.

After the first meeting, the hostess asked for a strategy session. She told the teacher, "You're talking language I don't understand. You'll have to learn a new lingo if you're going to reach me." The teacher could have been discouraged, but she didn't give up.

Two years later I went back to the same conference, and this couple wanted to take me to dinner. At the restaurant I saw twenty-six couples sitting around the table. My hosts said, "We thought you'd be interested in seeing the product of your ministry that day when you had six people in your workshop. These twenty-six couples have accepted Jesus Christ as their Saviour, and I want them to give their testimonies so you can hear them firsthand." One by one they gave their testimonies.

I thought as I listened how vital it is for Christians to discover how non-Christians think so our encounters can begin to communicate the truth of Jesus Christ.

MAINTAIN A "MODEL HOME"

Home Bible classes are an excellent way to evangelize our communities, but I think the greatest potential is in making our homes thoroughly Christian. Missionaries have told us for years that the greatest impact on a pagan society is made by the distinctively Christian home. It's evident that American culture is becoming pagan at an alarming rate. If Christian homes are distinctive and biblical, they will become more of a phenomenon every year in our degenerating society.

The wife of one of our seminary students has a responsible office position where twenty-two women work. Only five of these women have not been divorced, and most of the five are fed up with their marriages. "You begin to think you're an odd-wad because you are incredibly happy in your marriage," said the Christian. People watch to see how we relate to the problems of marriage, sickness, uncertainty, and death.

A couple in Fort Worth has a remarkable ministry they never asked God for. They have a boy who is dying of leukemia, and the community is watching to see if the Christian faith this couple has expressed really works. Do Christians crumble like pagans when death strikes?

I have a close friend who has six children, one of them mentally retarded. I love to visit that home because the reality of Jesus Christ is so attractively communicated. During family worship the older boy strums a chord on his little guitar, and off they go singing. This family is a light for God in their neighborhood because of their tender and realistic relationship with their children.

Genuine concern for members of the community comes naturally out of a home like that. I learned about a surgeon in Dallas who baffled his neighbors by his helpfulness. The doctor moved into a new neighborhood, and he looked out one day and saw his neighbor putting in grass. In Texas this means taking a piece of sod, cutting it into bits, and putting the little clumps in holes around the yard. He was doing this on a hot afternoon in August.

The doctor went over and said, "This is a hot day for a job like that; how about my giving you a hand?"

"Oh, no, Doc; I wouldn't expect you to do that."

"Let me help," the surgeon said, and he cut up the grass and started putting it in. They began talking, and after a while the lawn planter queried, "Say, I thought you were a surgeon."

"That's right, I am."

"Is planting sod good for surgeons?"

"I think so. Why?"

"Well, aren't you busy at the office—or what is your angle?"

"I don't have any angle," the doctor said. "I saw you putting this grass in and said to myself, 'That guy needs help; that's a big yard.'" So they went back to finishing the job.

A home Bible class began at the doctor's home recently, and afterward the neighbor who got help with his grass commented, "I just can't believe it!" He did, though, and ended up bringing twenty-seven other neighbors to the class!

In Philippians 2 we get Paul's insight into the mind of Christ. He says: "Let this mind be in you, which was also in Christ Jesus . . . who, being in the form of God . . . made Himself of no reputation, and took upon Him the form of a servant . . . and became obedient unto death, even the death of the cross" (vv. 5-8).

A little further on, Paul writes: "I trust . . . to send Timothy shortly unto you . . . for I have no man like-minded, who will naturally care for your state. For all seek their own, not the things of Jesus Christ" (vv. 19-21). Timothy, in Paul's large circle of friends, stood out as a man who was ready to serve, as the Lord Jesus Christ had done. This kind of unselfishness is so rare that it attracts a lot of attention—and questions—wherever it appears!

This service has to be genuine, however, or it will explode in our faces. Our neighbors may not want to hear about Jesus Christ, at least not right away, and time and testing will prove whether you really love your neighbor and are not simply seeking a trophy of your persuasive power.

USE STRATEGY

Another evangelism opportunity that few have taken advantage of is to invite friends and neighbors into your home to hear a "name" individual or a person who has an unusual story. We did this with a Cowboy football player, and the neighbors were so eager we probably could have charged admission!

The gridder really pounded our ears, and the "fans" were ready for more. More than that, the guest speaker enjoyed it so much he thought maybe he could start a Bible study group in his apartment building. I encouraged him, and by the end of the season he was teaching three classes every week. There are outstanding Christian people in every community who could attract neighbors to a home to hear an informal witness.

Some Christian families could have a fantastic foreign mission outreach without leaving their homes. More than 50,000 foreign students are studying in the United States, and they will hold influential positions in their countries when they return.

A Christian family in a university town was gathering information about Japan as a recreational project and asked a teacher at the university if he had any Japanese students. The teacher did, and arranged for two students to visit the family. In fact, they cooked the meal for the family, and everyone ate on the floor. It was a circus! Afterward the family invited the students to sit in on their family worship.

When the father was taking the students back to school, he

asked how long they had been in the U.S.

"Three years," they said.

"Have you ever been in a Christian home?"

"This was the first time," the students replied.

He had a natural opportunity then to tell them what Jesus Christ meant to his family. Maybe it was the first time they heard who Jesus really is. I hope it won't be the last.

INVOLVE YOUR WHOLE FAMILY

The greatest thing about making your home an evangelism center is the way it gets your whole family involved. Right after we moved into our former home, we bowed in the living room and dedicated the place to God as a base of operations for the community. I felt this was necessary because so many of my associations were with Christians, and we have to plan deliberately to make contacts with non-Christians.

We got our first opportunity quickly when an insurance broker moved across the street. I guess he just about moved out when he discovered he was living close to a preacher. He avoided me like the plague, but one day we ran into each other in the yard and I introduced myself. Jeanne and I took the initiative in building a friendship and didn't mention being Christians until many months later when a natural opening came during a time of need. I told him then what Christ had done for me, and my neighbor became my brother!

One of my favorite stories in the New Testament concerns the healing of the paralytic. His friends brought this cripple on a litter to see Jesus, but the place was so crowded they couldn't get in. That didn't stop them. They went up the side of the house to the roof and took it apart so they could lower the man right in front of Jesus. Mark reports: "And when He saw *their* faith, He said unto the sick of the palsy . . . Arise, and take up thy bed, and go thy way" (2:5, 9). It was a group effort that brought the man to Jesus, and I'm convinced that God honors a family group that takes on a project of reaching someone for Jesus Christ.

We got involved in a great experience with two of our children. The church planned a ski retreat between Christmas and New Year's, and the kids were to invite their unsaved friends to go. My two teenagers told us about the plan, and we started praying about it as a family. They ended up with eighteen kids for the trip, and we prayed every day for the venture.

On New Year's Eve we went to the church to welcome the returning buses. Looking for the familiar face of our daughter, we finally spotted her and saw her signal: ten fingers. Ten of those kids we prayed for had met Jesus as their Saviour on the retreat! That was a tremendous stimulus to the subsequent praying and witnessing of our family.

One of my sons became particularly interested in the ministry of camping. He spent a summer in Chicago taking kids camping on weekends and working during the week to support the project. A steady stream of kids met the Saviour.

When he came back to Dallas we talked about a ministry to kids there. I had been concerned about our Mexican-American community, for little evangelism was going on there. While some friends joined me in prayer, Christian kids went out and started building friendships.

One boy named Johnny was obviously the key to reaching many. He had the dubious distinction of stealing more cars in Dallas than any five criminals. Our young people built a relationship with Johnny, and he became a Christian. In order to arouse support for a further ministry, some of us arranged a luncheon for businessmen and asked Johnny to give his testimony. He said, "I ain't much for talking, but I'll sure tell them about Jesus."

I don't think he ever had a tie on before—he looked so uncomfortable at the luncheon. When it was his turn, he got up and said, "I'd rather do other things than talk, but I'd like to tell you that I came to know Jesus Christ as my Saviour. You 'wanta' know if it's for real? I'll tell you it's real: I'm *buying* my car."

The place erupted in laughter, and Johnny didn't quite know how to take it. He looked out over the audience and finally said: "If you don't think that takes a miracle, why should I buy a car when I can steal yours?" Then he looked at the group of Christian kids over at the table and said, "I'd like you to know that the only reason I came to know Jesus was because those kids over there cared."

That's the big issue before Christians today: Do we really care about the happiness and eternal destiny of our neighbors? If we do, we've got to do more than talk among Christians about their needs. We've got to go and live the Gospel among non-Christians!

LIVING THE MESSAGE
IN YOUR DAILY CONTACTS

Chapter Twelve

Professor Chad Walsh put it well in his intriguing book *Early Christians of the Twenty-first Century:* "Millions of Christians live in a sentimental haze of vague piety with soft organ music trembling in the lovely light from stained glass windows. Their religion is a pleasant thing of emotional quivers, divorced from the will, divorced from the intellect and demanding little except lip service to a few harmless platitudes. I suspect that Satan has called off his attempt to convert people to agnosticism. After all, if a man travels far enough away from Christianity, he is liable to see it in perspective and decide that it is true. It is much safer, from Satan's point of view, to vaccinate a man with a mild case of Christianity so as to protect him from the real disease."

No one could ever accuse the early church of being vaccinated with a mild case of Christianity. They had the "real disease" and it was communicable. They believed truth was not to be bottled, but dispensed. They were gripped and possessed of a message, one which had changed their lives and which they were convinced was able to change the lives of others. Their motto was: "We cannot but speak" (Acts 4:20).

Perhaps one of the reasons Christians do not witness today is that many of us have lost confidence in the power of the Gospel.

I had a third-year student at the seminary who told me one day, "Prof, I'm about to drop out." We talked for a while, and I realized Mike had lost confidence in his message. I told him: "It's been so long since you have seen the Gospel do something in someone's life that you've become an unbeliever in its potential. Why don't you ask God to give you a ministry in which you explode the Word of God in the life of people and see it work?" He agreed.

He was living in an apartment building alongside dental students, and he got a number of these students and their wives into a Bible class. One by one the couples came to know Christ as Saviour.

When Mike moved into his first year of graduate school, he started two other classes, one of which continued for about a year and a half. Then a group of prominent citizens invited him to conduct a class in one of their homes. One by one these people came to know Christ as their Saviour. Two of the men are executives in large corporations, and they meet with Mike each morning for Bible study and prayer before they go down to their offices which have become bases for evangelism. You can well imagine that Mike's confidence in the power of the Gospel is restored!

The Book of Acts makes it transparent that the message of the Gospel always has the same essential content, but the apostles used a variety of approaches to share their faith. I tell my students: "Die for your message, not your method."

Years ago I saw an ad for a product which read, "We couldn't improve our product so we improved the box." This is what I'm suggesting for communication of the Gospel: don't tamper with the message, but vary the package in which you present it. Presenting the Gospel is the act of saying the same truth in different ways to meet different needs in different situations.

A young wife in New England had recently discovered the su preme joy of knowing Jesus Christ, and she desperately wanted her husband to share this ecstasy. But as can so easily happen, she tried to cram the message down his throat. One night as they were preparing for bed, she was preaching away, quoting Bible verses, trying to persuade him to receive Christ. With a loving hug, he interrupted: "Aw, Honey, do I have to sleep with Billy Graham again?"

She got the point. From that time on she trusted the Lord for wisdom in living the message, in communicating the message in love. And you guessed it—in time he too received the abundant life offered by the Lord. What is it that Peter wrote? "Ye wives, be in subjection to your own husbands; that, if any obey not the Word, they also may without the Word be won by the conversation (manner of living) of the wives" (1 Peter 3:1).

Now I wouldn't condemn this young woman for her enthusiasm and persistence, but she was pushing it too far. And thankfully she got the message before she had built a wall between them.

Persistence has its place, however. But always it must be tempered with love and common sense. You can hammer away at a man for years, but if you do it just for the sake of winning a scalp you might as well forget it.

Ted DeMoss, a Chattanooga insurance broker, was a man who knew how to mix persistence with love. Once on a cold, rainy night he went out to call on a man who he had heard had a deep spiritual need. (Ted liked to call on nights like this; he usually found people at home!) It turned out that the man had moved away, so Ted, not one to pass up an opportunity, engaged the new resident in conversation. Ted soon uncovered one amazing fact: "I've been a Christian since the day I was born," the man told him. "My parents were Christians; so that made me a Christian." This man was a graduate engineer, and no dummy—but he obviously was totally ignorant of the way to God.

Over the next months Ted DeMoss prayed earnestly for this man, making more than twenty-five visits and contacts. Finally the man went with Ted to an evangelistic meeting; he went the next two evenings, and the third evening committed his life to Christ. It took over six months, but to DeMoss it was worth it. The next week, believe it or not, this man whom he had at last won was transferred to another state. God's timing was perfect!

As God was very much in charge of the episode involving Ted DeMoss and the engineer, you can be sure that He'll be in charge of your endeavors to communicate His message—if you'll put Him in charge. Be content to be the instrument and let Him determine how long it takes to strike gold. I believe with all my heart that "*today* is the day of salvation." But I also believe that the Lord is long-suffering; He doesn't do everything in a day. The seed the farmer plants may take many days to sprout, depending on how much rain and sunshine God sends. Be content to be workers together with Him. Maybe, in the long run, someone else will do the reaping. Just you be faithful in sowing the seed, be persistent, show love—and in time there will be reaping.

Some years ago in Philadelphia, the George sisters—five unmarried women of Armenian descent—literally reached out in love to a hurting big city world—and then sat back and let God work in hearts. Frequently they had guests in for dinner to show kindness—and to share God's love as revealed in Jesus Christ. People learned that there was a family that cared, and as one result, the phone rang day and night; often callers needed counsel, comfort, encouragement.

Once Mary George was on the phone when an operator interrupted with an emergency call. Moments later Mary, just a ninety-pound slip of a woman, was on her way to Philadelphia General Hospital to be at the bedside of a former neighbor who had been found on her kitchen floor badly burned. This woman, whom I'll call Miss White, had lived next door to the Georges and had fallen on hard times, becoming a recluse after her family passed away. Her house had become almost unlivable, the odor nauseating. Miss White herself looked like her house—dirty and unkept. The Georges had heard of her situation and had gone to her aid, taking her food and clothing from time to time. Once, Virginia, the youngest sister, wrecked her car as she reached for a cake sliding on the seat beside her; the cake was for Miss White.

Early in their contact, the Georges discovered that Miss White seemed bitter toward God. He had taken her family and left her alone, she complained. But they didn't scold; they simply witnessed of God's love and concern and spoke of God's love in sending Christ to bear her sins. They took her to church and to a Bible conference in the Poconos.

After many years, just before the accident in her kitchen, Miss White's attitude toward God changed, and she trusted Christ. Thus, at the hospital Mary George was able to comfort her from the Word, to pray with her and remind her that Christ was with her. Soon Miss White died, and the George sisters had complete charge of her funeral. No relatives showed up. Mary, in recounting the story, said, "Often as we ministered to her in life, and then in death, we were reminded of the words of Matthew 25:40—'Inasmuch as ye have done it unto one of the least of these My brethren, ye have done it unto Me.'"

That is love in action. This family has, in God's power, learned to say it with love in the City of Brotherly Love.

There are countless opportunities to stand in the gap for God, and that's all He really expects us to do. If we are on His wavelength, He will show us by His Spirit how we can touch a life for Him. He will show us the right way to say it and when to say it. Sharon Weese, of Camp Point, Illinois had casually on several occasions invited her friend Judy to church but had gotten nowhere. Judy and her husband had attended church before their marriage, but now they couldn't agree on which church to attend; so they went nowhere. One day Sharon touched a vital nerve when she said to Judy: "Don't you want Christ to be part of Greg's character?"

Judy thought of her little son, and finally sighed, "I know you're right, Sharon, but I don't know if Don will agree to go to your church."

But Sunday morning Judy, Don and little Greg were in church. The second Sunday both parents took that small step of faith and joined the family of God—because of an extra nudge given in love and a word spoken in season. Sharon's concern had paid off.

I have a friend named Jim who is sort of a low-key witness—but he has found that concern and friendship are important in communicating Christ. He made a point to talk to the high school kid, Bob, who mowed his lawn, though rapping with a high schooler wasn't really his cup of tea. The kid was a rail fan—a *locomaniac*—and Jim made it a point to talk trains with him. He hardly knew a 2-6-0 Mogul from a 4-8-8-4 Big Boy, but he learned from Bob.

Even after Bob chucked his lawn mower and went to a local college, he dropped in from time to time to talk with Jim. They had become friends, and Jim had a listening ear. Occasionally talk would shift to matters relating to eternal life. Jim still doesn't know when Bob crossed the line, but he told someone else that Jim had led him to Christ. Bob later attended seminary and now serves overseas.

You can find ways of showing love and concern wherever you find yourself—at home, in your neighborhood, in the marketplace, on the street. Tommy Morris has mastered that difficult art of balancing trays while waiting tables in a dining car on a passenger train run between Chicago and Seattle. He has also mastered the art of relating to people—and being guided by the Holy Spirit. He makes a point of doing Gospel work at both ends of his run.

Once in Seattle he was about to distribute Gospel tracts on a street corner, but somehow he couldn't. He began walking—where, he didn't know. A man stopped him; he was hungry, just out of the penitentiary, he said. Tommy took him into a restaurant and bought him a hearty meal. As the man dined, Tommy counseled, "I want to tell you about a Friend that sticks closer than a brother. I'm going to tell you about Someone you should turn to in this hour. I don't care what you've done. Man may fail you, but the Lord Jesus Christ shed His blood for you to save you if you'll let Him inside your heart."

A little later, Tommy took the man to the Bread of Life Mission, where he committed his life to Christ after responding to the invitation in the Gospel service there. Tommy counseled him in the prayer room. But it wasn't until he heard the man testify in another service that he realized how definitely he had been led by the Holy Spirit. The man revealed, "I was on my way to commit suicide when a man spoke to me and brought me in and pointed me to the Saviour."

In North Platte, Nebraska, Paul Flaming teaches English at the high school, and he lets Christ shine from his life. Christ has permeated his life, and His philosophy spills out. "I find that I have many opportunities to witness for Christ around school," Flaming says, "and if I use good judgment in where and when I talk about the Lord, I have no fear of getting into trouble for it.

"When you deal in class with Golding's *Lord of the Flies*," he says, "you deal with the fact that man is basically evil. When you teach Hardy's *The Mayor of Casterbridge*, you are dealing with character. How big a part of character is true Christianity!

"And, of course, all the recommended English courses say Milton's *Paradise Lost* should be taught," he continues. "The Christian English teacher who can't find an effective way to witness through that masterpiece has something wrong with his Christian experience."

But the most effective witness, Flaming says, is with one student at a time, by taking natural opportunities to speak for Christ.

Connie came in to discuss her term paper and the subject of philosophy came up. Flaming had the chance to tell her his philosophy of life. When a Gospel movie showed in North Platte, he bought a number of tickets and gave them to students. There Connie made her decision for Christ.

I am convinced the world is more eager to hear our message than we are to deliver it. Never in my ministry have I seen such responsiveness and receptivity to the Gospel as in recent days.

A Lutheran church in Minneapolis put a slogan on billboards, sides of buses, and elsewhere that read: "I love you"; it was signed, "Jesus"; and under it the question: "Is that OK?" We're living in a depersonalized society in which many people are asking: "Does anyone care?"

In ancient Palestine our Lord encountered a woman who had bled constantly for years. Mark records that she approached Him in a crowd, and Jesus didn't miss her. He could discern between the indiscriminate press of a mob and her touch of faith. Can we?

As I study the Scriptures, I see that there are only two things God wants to rescue from this deteriorating planet. One is His Word, and the other is people. Are you investing your life in these treasures God is going to save? Are you building His Word into people? Invest your life in something that will outlast you!

Recently I ran across a quotation that stabbed me: "There was never a feast without a sacrifice." This was true for Christ who "came not to be ministered unto, but to minister, and to give His life a ransom for many" (Matt. 20:28). It is also true for believers who die to themselves so they may bear Christ to the hungry souls of the world.

A MESSAGE TO SHARE
(with love)...

How To Live Forever...

and have a meaningful life right now.

Some people think

that to live forever and enjoy a meaningful life now a person must:

- help others
- go to church
- get to the top
- have friends
- be healthy and happy
- make plenty of money

All of these make sense in a way...

but

we all know people who do these things and life is still incomplete.

WHY?

Because life consists of more than just these things. They do not give us a right relationship with God, the source of life.

Here are four facts we need to know....

1 A meaningful life begins with God!

Jesus said:
"God so loved the world, that He gave His only begotten Son, that whoever believes in Him should not perish, but have everlasting life."   John 3:16

Jesus also said:
"I have come that they might have life, and that they might have it more abundantly."   John 10:10

Augustine observed:
"Thou has made us for Thyself, O God, and the heart of man is restless until it finds its rest in Thee."

According to the Bible,
look what God offers you:

Love—Someone who cares about you.

Security—Someone who cares about what happens to you.

Peace—Someone who cares about your problems

Purpose—Someone who cares about whether your life counts.

Eternal life—Someone who cares about your future.

UNFORTUNATELY...

---
2 Our sin separates us from God.

The Bible says:
"All of us, like sheep, have gone astray; we have turned, every one of us, to his own way."   Isaiah 53:6

According to the Bible sin is:

- Failure to be what God wants us to be
- Failure to do what God wants us to do

Obviously then, all of us have sinned.
Consciously or unconsciously we
have rebelled against God.

That's not all.
The penalty of sin is death.   **S**
God is righteous so   **I**
He must judge sin.   **N**

"The wages of sin is death."   Romans 6:23

"Your sins have been a barrier between you and your God."
                                                            Isaiah 59:2

As long as sin separates us from God, we cannot enjoy the meaningful life now or eternal life with God in heaven.

FORTUNATELY...

> **3   God loves you very much! He gave Jesus Christ, His Son, to take away your sin.**

The Bible says:
"God showed His love toward us, in that, while we were yet sinners, Christ died for us."

Romans 5:8

"Christ died for our sins ... and arose again the third day."

1 Corinthians 15:3-4

God is satisfied with what Jesus Christ has done. Now He is free to forgive you and to offer you eternal life with Him.

Jesus Christ has removed the barrier of sin through His death.

However, you must respond.

---

4   To have a meaningful life now and eternal life with God, you must trust Jesus Christ to forgive your sins.

Look at what the Bible tells us:

"Jesus said, I am the way, the truth, and the life: no man comes to the Father, but by Me."   John 14:6

"Believe on the Lord Jesus Christ and you will be saved." Acts 16:31

"Being justified [set right with God] by faith, we have peace with God through our Lord Jesus Christ."   Romans 5:1

But what is faith?

We exercise faith when we

- **Depend** on a doctor
- **Trust** in a lawyer
- **Rely** on a friend

Faith in the Lord Jesus Christ, therefore, is trusting Him to forgive your sins and to bring you into a right relationship with God.

Let's review..

You know that...

A meaningful life begins with God. Your sin separates you from God. Jesus Christ, by His death, provides forgiveness for your sin.

The only thing God asks you to do:

Trust the Lord Jesus Christ to forgive your sins.

Are you still here?   Or have you trusted
                            Jesus Christ
                    completely to forgive your sins?

Wouldn't you like to trust Jesus Christ to forgive your sins right now?

You may want to use this prayer to express your decision:

"Dear Father, I admit that I am a sinner. I believe that the Lord Jesus Christ died for me. I trust Jesus Christ to forgive my sins right now. Thank You for the gift of eternal life with You. Amen."

To experience fully the benefits of this new life, you need to grow in Christ. Here are some suggestions for spiritual growth:

You need to study the Bible daily to become aware of what God wants to do for you and with you.
Read 1 Peter 2:2.

As a Christian, Christ's Spirit now indwells you. Power to do what the Word of God says comes as you rely on the Holy Spirit. *Read Galatians 5:16.*

Prayer is a vital privilege for the person who has trusted Christ. Speak to God often about your needs. *Read Philippians 4:6-7.*

One more thing. It's difficult to be a Christian alone. Meet with others who have trusted the Lord Jesus Christ in a church where the Bible is taught. *Read Hebrews 10:25.*